100 Questions (and Answers) About Action Research

Q&A SAGE 100 Questions and Answers Series

1. *100 Questions (and Answers) About Research Methods,* by Neil J. Salkind

2. *100 Questions (and Answers) About Tests and Measurement,* by Bruce B. Frey

3. *100 Questions (and Answers) About Statistics,* by Neil J. Salkind

4. *100 Questions (and Answers) About Qualitative Research,* by Lisa M. Given

5. *100 Questions (and Answers) About Research Ethics,* by Emily E. Anderson and Amy Corneli

6. *100 Questions (and Answers) About Survey Research,* by Erin Ruel

7. *100 Questions (and Answers) About Action Research,* by Luke Duesbery and Todd Twyman

Visit **sagepub.com/100qa** for a current listing of titles in this series.

100 Questions (and Answers) About Action Research

Luke Duesbery
San Diego State University

Todd Twyman
Pacific University

Los Angeles | London | New Delhi
Singapore | Washington DC | Melbourne

FOR INFORMATION:

SAGE Publications, Inc.
2455 Teller Road
Thousand Oaks, California 91320
E-mail: order@sagepub.com

SAGE Publications Ltd.
1 Oliver's Yard
55 City Road
London EC1Y 1SP
United Kingdom

SAGE Publications India Pvt. Ltd.
B 1/I 1 Mohan Cooperative Industrial Area
Mathura Road, New Delhi 110 044
India

SAGE Publications Asia-Pacific Pte. Ltd.
18 Cross Street #10-10/11/12
China Square Central
Singapore 048423

Printed in the United States of America

Library of Congress Cataloging-in-Publication Data

Names: Duesbery, Luke, author. | Twyman, Todd, author.

Title: 100 questions (and answers) about action research / Luke Duesbery, Todd Twyman.

Other titles: One hundred questions (and answers) about action research

Description: Los Angeles : SAGE, 2020. | Series: Q&A Sage 100 questions and answers series ; 7 | Includes index.

Identifiers: LCCN 2018052664 | ISBN 9781544305431 (pbk. : alk. paper)

Subjects: LCSH: Action research. | Action research in education. | Action research in public health.

Classification: LCC H62 .D795 2020 | DDC 001.4—dc23
LC record available at https://lccn.loc.gov/2018052664

This book is printed on acid-free paper.

Acquisitions Editor: Helen Salmon
Editorial Assistant: Megan O'Heffernan
Production Editor: Jyothi Sriram
Copy Editor: Lana Arndt
Typesetter: C&M Digitals (P) Ltd.
Proofreader: Sarah Duffy
Indexer: Sylvia Coates
Cover Designer: Candice Harman
Marketing Manager: Shari Countryman

SUSTAINABLE FORESTRY INITIATIVE
Certified Chain of Custody
At Least 10% Certified Forest Content
www.sfiprogram.org
SFI-01028

19 20 21 22 23 10 9 8 7 6 5 4 3 2 1

Contents

Preface

The genesis of this book stems from the authors' personal experiences.

For Todd Twyman, it was with his oldest son, Ian. Todd tells the story of how Ian came home in tears at the end of the first week of school because he was in a reading group that was studying letters (alphabetic awareness). At this point, Ian was already able to read chapter books, and while Todd is not a reading expert, he is an expert in research and assessment. At his first parent–teacher conference, Todd asked Ian's teacher why he was not assigned to a more appropriate group. The response was that "he scored below grade level on the test of oral reading fluency [ORF]." An ORF test asks a child to read for a minute, and then the number of correct words read is counted. And while the placement decision made sense from a data standpoint, it was obviously not the appropriate placement. When Todd asked about Ian's scores on the other four measures of reading (alphabetic awareness, phonemic segmentation, vocabulary, and comprehension), the teacher reported that Ian scored at the *top* of his class in *all* of those measures. Ian was a good reader, but maybe not a fast one. Really, what parent teaches their child to read fast? Unfortunately, Ian would have to wait until the next cycle of testing before being reassigned. After Todd's partner talked him off the metaphorical ledge, he approached Ian's teacher as both a father and action researcher. Look at the data, try something different, are you sure? The teacher was actually relieved to have support. This is what action research is about—openly thinking and making decisions with one another.

For Luke Duesbery, it was with his daughter, Tiegue. In third grade, Tiegue was asked to complete a research project for the school science fair. You probably know of the standard elementary school science fairs. One hundred children packed into the gymnasium with poster boards and explaining what they had done over the semester. Given Luke's background in research methodology, he volunteered to be a judge. His daughter's project involved giving half of her class chocolate before reading a passage, to see if they read faster. Her hypothesis was that caffeine, via chocolate, could improve scores. Yes, the same test of ORF Todd described in the previous paragraph. It was a clever study. She knew chocolate could make your mind race, and she knew the test was about speed. Seeing her project and the simple and elegant projects the other elementary students generated caused Luke to question if there are real and smaller questions we can all answer like the third graders do?

Throughout our careers, we have been fortunate to work with many professionals—teachers, nurses, policymakers, CEOs, parents, and students from the kindergarten to graduate level. Our experiences are what drive this book. We believe there is a fundamental need for all of us to understand how action research can improve lives. And although much has been written about action research from different lenses—for example, systems and accountability, leadership, field practice—little has been written about action research as a form of advocacy and more specifically as a form of social justice. Thus, this book does not follow the path of textbooks that tacitly support the status quo. Rather, it is our intent that this book serve as a reference for readers to improve their practice as advocates for those they serve, their community, and—along the way—their children.

In this book, we choose not to clutter the text with citations. Instead we provide an appendix with what we think are books and articles worth pursuing, should you be interested.

—Live action research for life, not the day.

Acknowledgments

The authors would like to collectively acknowledge their partners, Fatima and Nancy. Both put up with our writing retreats, and both provided guidance in writing this book. Of course, all of our children had to put up with us, too: Tiegue, Ian, Cohen, and Scott. Thanks to Helen Salmon at SAGE, who kept the fire burning over the long writing process. And lastly, our respect goes out to Neil Salkind, without whose vision this book would never exist.

The authors and SAGE would like to thank the following reviewers for their feedback:

Eva M. Moya, University of Texas at El Paso

Shannon Cleverly-Thompson, St. John Fisher College

Caryn E. Saxon, Missouri State University

Sarah Garner, Southeast Missouri State University

Jacquelynn Doyon-Martin, Grand Valley State University

Rebecca Herr Stephenson, Loyola Marymount University

Jennifer Keahey, Arizona State University

About the Authors

Luke Duesbery is an Associate Professor at San Diego State University, where he has taught in the Departments of Special Education and Teacher Education for more than 10 years. Before that, he was a classroom teacher in both Virginia and Oregon in multiple subject areas and multiple grades. His interest is in bridging the gap between research and practice. His areas of research include understanding research though graphical representations of data, critical thinking and creativity, measurement, and alternative and innovative research methods, such as action research.

Todd Twyman is an Associate Professor in the School of Learning and Teaching at Pacific University, where he primarily teaches action research. He was a high school social studies teacher in San Francisco prior to earning his PhD at the University of Oregon, where he specialized in tests and measurement. His research interests include test development and bridging the research-to-practice gap.

What Is Action Research?

Action research offers a greatly needed forum at a time of growing recognition around the world that engagements between researchers and practitioners are central to generating both new knowledge and innovations.

—L. David Brown

What Is This Book About?

The world of research can seem complicated, especially when you first start learning about it. There is no shortage of books one can read and classes one can take about research, but somehow, they miss the mark in many ways. There should be some way to learn the fundamentals, in simple terms, as you enter into that world of research. This book is about those fundamentals. It is not an "idiot's" or "dummy's" guide to action research. It simply organizes and delivers the 100 most relevant questions and answers to help you get the lay of the land. The jargon, concepts, and facts to have a good understanding of what matters in action research are distilled into digestible language.

Action research is not like traditional research, it is younger, more dynamic, and more relevant to us in our daily practice. Action research encompasses a philosophy of work and learning, while also providing us with critical know-how to better our lives and our work, and also better the lives of those we work with and for.

There are 10 parts in this book. Each one can stand alone, but we hope you move through them sequentially to a get a better idea of the big picture. Parts 1 and 2 lay the groundwork and address questions about what it means to be an action researcher. Part 3 provides concrete examples of action research in the field. Parts 4 through 7 cover the nuts and bolts of doing action research. Part 8 covers details about sharing and communicating results, and Parts 9 and 10 take you beyond practice and out into the action research world.

In this book, you are going to learn how action research can help you change your life and career for the better. It is a way of thinking about measuring, quantifying, adjusting, and thinking about decisions that really matter. We aren't interested in reading volumes about research methods; we are interested in getting things done, and getting them done efficiently, systematically, and with purpose. Ultimately, the choice to make change—to act—is ours.

More questions? See question 100.

What Is Action Research, and Where Did It Come From?

S imply put, action research is a method of systematically examining behavior in an effort to improve practice. The *action* refers to doing something. The *research* refers to thinking critically and logically about a problem. Together, they form a powerful combination for making productive change in the workplace.

Action research was originally coined by Kurt Lewin in the late 1940s and has evolved into an umbrella term for any systematic approach bridging research and practice by empowering practitioners with decision-making authority. Basically, action research allows those who live the issue to be the main participant in systematically solving the issue. Action research creates an ability to delve into complex issues in any given situation through formal investigation.

This idea is not new. It was primarily used early on by social scientists in the United States who explored issues in business and communities (i.e., wage disparity, sociocultural discrimination). Noted American educators such as Hilda Taba and John Dewey early in the 20th century used action research principles as tools for teachers to link what they were seeing and doing in their classrooms to what more controlled research was reporting, but in a more applicable and meaningful way. And while action research fell out of favor in the United States with ivory tower positivists who believed that only experts conducted valuable research to answer universal "truths," teachers in Great Britain continued to use action research well into the 1960s. And so, while its roots lay in a strong qualitative tradition, action research has changed and grown over time to be more aptly called a mixed-method approach, borrowing from both qualitative and quantitative traditions.

In the 1970s, arguably as an extension of Paulo Freire's anti-colonial view of education, this "new" theoretical approach, combined with the narrowing rift between seemingly conflicting qualitative and quantitative research traditions in education, provided necessary pushback to positivist researchers. In its current iteration, considering the fact that practitioners are critical pieces in reform, action research is looked upon as a piece of workplace development and individual professional development.

Other popular names for action research are *participatory action research, practical inquiry, teacher research, practitioner research, reflective inquiry, inquiry-oriented teaching,* or other similarly phrased compound words including synonyms for research and practice. And while the actual label may be confusing, at the heart of the matter is the fact that we are all naturally researchers, perhaps without knowing it. We often try out new strategies and make changes and modifications based on "how it worked" in our daily lives. Action research formalizes this intuition.

More questions? See questions 4, 7, and 21.

What Are the Key Features of Action Research I Should Remember?

There are many kinds of research, each coming from slightly different perspectives. Some of these differences arise because research spans all fields, and some just because of internal differences of opinion. The core for most of these research perspectives is, for the most part, the same. For example, in both traditional and action research, developing a high-quality research question is important. The difference lies in how and why the question is shaped. Also, many of the approaches used in action research look similar to program evaluation research, but subtle differences arise, like the subject of focus and scope. In program evaluation, the subject of interest is a multifaceted entity: Many research questions are posed, and research is typically conducted by an outsider(s). In action research, one or a few questions are posed about a relatively small sample of participants by someone who is deeply involved with the research. Although there are differences in research traditions, there are key features of action research that make it unique.

Action Research	Traditional Research
Focuses on a single setting	Focuses on larger scales
Uses the sample of interest, the people you work with or know	Seeks to randomly select participants
Is more informal and dynamic	Seeks to use rigorous methodology over long-term studies
Tends to rely on easy-to-access descriptive measures	Demands sophisticated statistical analysis
Looks to inform practice	Looks to inform theory
Requires less formal training	Requires an advanced degree or specialized training

Even if these key features don't make sense or mean a lot to you now, rest assured when you have finished this book, they will make perfect sense.

More questions? See questions 4, 9, and 10.

How Is Action Research Like and Unlike Other Research?

I n formal or traditional research, no matter the field, a driving concern is generalizability. This means that results from a study, let's say with a small group of people, apply to a larger group of people. For example, if you wanted to know if a medical procedure designed to alleviate symptoms of Alzheimer's worked well, you would not need to try it on *everyone* with Alzheimer's. Instead, you would test the innovation on a few and generalize to the larger population. If it works with a group of 50 people, then maybe it will work with 5 million people. Again, this is an objective of traditional, or positivist, research. From a small *sample* of people, data are generalized to a larger *population* of people. With traditional research, you would need to worry about complex issues related to the size and makeup of the group and whether they can represent the population.

With action research, you are not usually interested in a larger population. In a small business, you might be interested in how your local customers respond to a new product. This is the defining difference with action research—generalizability can be important, but not a priority. You are working under the assumption that your group, whether patients, customers, or students, remains similar from year to year. And so, what you find out this year will likely be the same as next year, and the year after that. The defining characteristic of action research is that *you* are the researcher, and *you* are interested in doing something to benefit *your* context. It is personal. Action research puts the *you* in research.

More questions? See questions 2, 21, and 37.

How Do You Choose Your Action Research Style?

Technical action research, practical action research, and critical action research are three different and generally agreed-upon types of action research. *How do you choose?* Answering questions about your project will dictate the type, or style, of action research you use. For example, does the action research project intend to examine the effectiveness of a "new" or "adaptive" practice? Or does the action research project intend to change the existing working workplace culture? Answers to these may seem rudimentary, but they are critical to choosing the appropriate style of action research.

- **Technical action research** asks you to apply an existing practice from somewhere else and test its effectiveness in your setting. Technical action research is probably the most widely used, as it addresses some current issue for which there is an offered solution. Technical action research also more closely follows traditional research design protocols (e.g., group comparison designs) and attends to internal validity more than other types (i.e., control for extraneous variables). For example, perhaps a plant manager notices inefficiency or a preponderance of errors in the accounting department. He or she then goes to a trade show and sees a new piece of accounting software espoused to cut time and increase productivity. The technical action research project would compare the outcome variables across time to judge the software developers' claims. Technical action research is typically an either/or proposition. In the example, the software works or it doesn't.

- **Practical action research** differs from technical action research in that you *design* the changes, not merely adopt an existing practice.

- **Critical action research** changes the game in that you want to change existing structures and actively engage in changing the "system," by working with or against other participants in the same context.

All three styles can be used in combination. Typically, action research projects start on the technical side, as it addresses an immediate observed issue. However, because all contexts are individual, existing programs don't necessarily generalize. There are many different participants and structures that require some sort of adaptation.

More questions? See questions 37, 38, 39, and 40.

Why Should I Bother With Action Research?

Because it's important, and here's why. Todd was a public high school social studies teacher in San Francisco, California. It was a challenging school with high student mobility, consistent staff turnover, extremely limited access to resources, a district policy that forced students to go away from their neighborhood school without providing transportation, and oh by the way, statewide test scores were extraordinarily low when compared to other public schools in the city. Todd figured the best way to address these issues was to roll up his sleeves and get to work giving the best education he could to those he served. Of course, you say. That's what good teachers do. But how do you address these issues? What can you teach that will get kids interested enough to come and stay in school, while raising test scores and not driving you crazy enough to quit in the middle of the year? Sounds daunting, but it's really not, and action research can help. Fortunately, Todd hung out with a couple of lawyers that were looking for volunteer hours as part of their job. Todd mentioned that the district had a mock trial competition every year, and that would be a nice symbiotic relationship. The lawyers got their volunteer hours, and Todd got the badly needed help. In their first year, students from this high school won the district mock trial championship and traveled to the state championship. It is a good story, but was it really effective? Did it improve the concerning issues of the school?

Here's where action research came in. Todd noticed an increase in attendance, engagement, and classroom test scores. Coincidence? Not after 4 years of similar outcome patterns. The mock trial built community, increased academic interest, and gave everyone a vested voice. And, yes, statewide test scores increased for those student participants; a nice byproduct. That is the real improvement any teacher worth her or his salt wants: community, engagement, and voice for improvement. Whatever position you hold, or wherever you work, think about something you really want to change, ask a good question, document it, and act.

More questions? See questions 2, 77, and 88.

How Is Action Research Cyclical?

I t begins, and it never ends. This is true with action research, and with learning in general. Think about it. When you get smarter about something, you are naturally led to new questions, new curiosities, and then more answers. Let us illustrate what an Action Research Cycle (ARC) looks like.

Figure 1.1

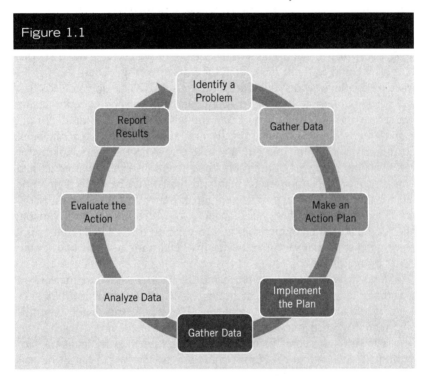

The ARC begins as you identify a problem and shape it into a question or hypothesis statement. Most often, it is a question of whether or not some innovation works, and upon what it might depend. For example, perhaps you notice a problem at work. In this identification stage the action researcher would probably seek advice from others, or perhaps Google the problem to see what others are doing about it. Identifying the problem, and thus your research question and hypothesis, is the first stage in the ARC.

Most often, the next step is to gather data. In some cases, your question will already be based on sound data, and gathering more is unnecessary. In schools, many teachers will use student outcome data, like quizzes, tests, or grades. Some might choose observable behaviors like attendance, referrals, and so on. Still others may choose to create a survey or questionnaire to gather data. Health care workers will use patient well-being inventories. Entrepreneurs will likely be concerned with employee and customer satisfaction and, ultimately, profit. The question identified often dictates the kind of data you will use. For example, perhaps a teacher recognizes students are not doing their homework. Then the question identified might be

Will checking homework as students enter class improve the homework completion rate?

For this example, the data collected are determined by the research question. The need now is to determine how often students do their homework. The action plan is a written procedure of what, when, and how you will do something. This is an important step because it forces you to think through contingencies before you implement a plan. In this step, you operationalize your thinking and make it concrete.

When you implement the plan, you are taking note of anything out of the ordinary that happens that might unduly influence the result.

Either during or after the *action*, you will again gather data. In the homework example, you were gathering data throughout the action. In other situations, you may find yourself having to collect data after some intervention or change.

Now that you have your data, you will need to analyze them. This is where you turn data into usable information. Data alone do not help decision making. Did it work for everyone? Are there some groups it did not work for? As you compile the information and reflect on the results you are naturally led to deeper questions. You are led back to the beginning to reshape your thoughts now that you've learned something.

While not an absolutely necessary component of the cycle, we recommend action researchers also take the time to report results. This might be as simple as sharing with a colleague or as ambitious as publishing the research in a professional journal.

More questions? See 6 and 8.

How Much Time Does an Action Research Project Really Take?

Y ou will read this phrase throughout this book: *It depends*. The duration of an action research project really does depend on many different elements, like your question, skill set, participant availability, and so on. All of these are covered in more detail in this book. For example, imagine that you are a teacher and want to know if there is a difference between females and males in your class on statewide test scores for math. All you would need to do is to pull your students' scores from the state database and then analyze the data. Similarly, if you are a social worker you might want to add a question or two to your mental health intake paperwork and then look at the responses. Both are pretty quick projects, maybe 3 hours each. Not too bad, but what does it really get you? Not much, except those answers could be an entrée to forming more complex questions.

To continue with the examples, let's say males outscore females on these tests, or that mental health clients are suspicious of giving out their personal information. As a teacher or mental health professional, you want to change these circumstances. For either discipline, the process is the same. You would search the literature for effective interventions (~4 hours), implement changes during a specified time frame (~10 hours total), collect and structure data (~5 hours), analyze data (~4 hours), and report out your findings (~2 hours). In sum, about 25 hours. Seems like a lot, so you are probably saying that there is no way you can do that in the normal scope of your work. You would be right, and we wouldn't recommend that. However, throughout this book, we discuss ways to integrate action research into your daily routine, not add to it. Further, when you become facile in integrating action research into your daily work life, you will find that you become a more inquisitive and effective practitioner with what we call an *action research disposition*. This disposition is an approach to asking and answering questions of the world, and it lasts a lifetime.

More questions? See questions 5, 6, and 7.

What Is an Action Research Disposition?

G ot a question? Need an answer? Action research is ideal for the person who enjoys inquiry. An inquiry-oriented disposition begins with posing questions instead of stating facts. Those with an inquiry-oriented disposition understand that answers depend on many things. This stands in stark contrast to the traditional positivist research disposition, which holds that there are universal truths that might be applied in all situations. While this is of course appealing to our sense of order and need for structure, an action research disposition admits that we cannot know all.

A close parallel across disciplines might be problem-based learning (PBL). A PBL paradigm is situated within a scenario that needs some kind of resolution. To be clear, in action research, we do not research out of curiosity; we conduct research because we need and want to make change.

Action researchers are curious, but also driven. We are open to suggestions, but also eager to implement action. We are logical with planning, skeptical of "what research says." So much of what is thought to be known entirely *depends* on context.

For example, traditional research tells us that a vaccination for polio is most effective when applied at a young age and that vaccination should be repeated at ideal intervals to optimize effectiveness. That same research does not tell us why the vaccination might not work. In a population with high levels of seasonal migration, where follow-up vaccinations are unlikely, is single vaccination effective? Do the benefits of single vaccination outweigh the risks of side effects? We might investigate the deployment of a modified vaccination schedule that looks closely at a local population, instead of relying on ideals and averages.

Action researchers are, above all, flexible and reflective. Local data, local context, and local control. Action researchers take meaningful actions that lead to better understanding and knowledge. Action researchers do not ignore traditional research findings. We take it with a grain—no, a dash—of salt.

More questions? See questions 10, 21, and 22.

Why Is Knowing Yourself Important While Doing Action Research?

You come to your graduate program or workplace with preconceptions about how the world works and your place in it. So, it's critical to understand facts and ideas in the context of a conceptual framework and organize knowledge in ways that facilitate retrieval and action. Self-reflection in action research can help you learn to take control of your own learning.

Action research settings are complicated, and engaging in action research happens within a shared environment. Cognitive anthropologists Jean Lave and Etienne Wenger (1991) refer to this as a *community of practice*, where people come together with common interests and goals to improve their situation. However, the notion of "common" is up to the individual and can at times be in conflict with others in that community. So, knowing yourself and your place in that shared environment can impact the success or failure of achieving a particular goal.

If we agree that knowledge is best gained through multiple voices and perspectives, then we must also recognize the strength of identity development in the context of diversity and equity, as part and parcel to examining problems of practice. Action research is particularly powerful in supporting our learning, negotiating, and (re)interpreting the often-conflicting conversations that are situated in and among places of power.

The term *reflexivity* is often used in action research. It is found in several fields, such as adult learning, work-based practice, and more specifically, qualitative research based on the 1970s works of Argyris and Schön. Reflexivity happens when we acknowledge that our history and identity impact our research. With respect to action research, reflexivity refers to our self-awareness in the sense that when we conduct an action research project, we are more concerned with seeing our truth as it relates to our place in the world. We aren't necessarily concerned that our action research findings generalize to the greater world, but how our results impact the work we do, how we are transformed by them, and how our research benefits all stakeholders.

Here's why it's important: When we acknowledge that our participation in action research is subjective by nature, we can work to know our social world more effectively. For example, we assume many things are "normal" or "common sense." However, normality is in the eye of the beholder. In other words, normal might be being straight, White, and male. Of course, this shouldn't be the case, but it often is. Once we examine that these are actually potential biases, we can begin to work toward a more equitable and ethical framework to minimize power dynamics that exist (teacher to student, doctor to patient, manager to employee).

More questions? See questions 21 and 22.

Do I Need to Know About Statistics for Action Research?

Because generalizability is not your priority, you will have little need for complicated statistics, although we present common statistical approaches in Part 8. Unlike traditional experimental research, with action research, you make change and observe the impact on your entire group of interest. You will not need to generalize from your sample to a broader population. Instead you generalize from your sample to a similar sample of people.

With action research, you are also interested in quickly making changes based on results. Traditional research might work in grand cycles of years where the investigator slowly and methodically examines an issue in depth. In contrast, action research is quick and dynamic. When a teacher tries a new math program, and it doesn't work after 3 months, they might make a change before the start of next semester, all the while collecting data to inform decision making. If an entrepreneur develops a new marketing program, and there is little response after a month, they make an immediate change.

However, with action research, you are still interested in asking meaningful questions and gathering high-quality data. And so, like with traditional research, you need to define variables well, identify and describe a target population with precision, and design a methodology and collect data to ensure results are valid.

Action research typically encompasses projects that are informal and directed at improving some practice, whether in a classroom, at a bank, or in a hospital. While action research might use many of the same methods as formal research found in laboratories and universities, it is not typical. The focus of formal research is to discover broadly what can be applied in all settings, whereas action research is typically focused on a single discrete setting. Much of this book is devoted to these topics, so please, read on.

More questions? See questions 37, 66, 69, 70, and 74.

Preparing for Action Research

*Appeals to justice still have the power
to awaken a moral imagination and motivate
people to look at their society critically, to
ask how it can be made more liberating and
enabling.*

—**Iris Marion Young**

12

What's the Difference Between Theory and Conceptual Frameworks in Action Research?

Theory and conceptual frameworks sound similar, and indeed they are. However, they mean different things in different contexts, which is particularly important to science. In metaphysical terms, a concept is something that fundamentally exists, like the concept of gravity. It is an abstract idea thought to explain why things fall to the ground, or to explain why we don't float away. On the other hand, a theory is something that is tested to explain a certain phenomenon, like why someone behaves in a certain way. Think intrinsic and extrinsic motivation as theories to explain why someone works hard, or not. Theories are typically used to challenge and extend existing assumptions about certain observed phenomena.

To confuse matters, gravity could be considered a theory, but here's the difference. As a concept, gravity is some force that just is. As a theory, gravity can be tested to prove or disprove its legitimacy with a bunch of observations in an effort to prove its existence. Here are a few ways to figure out if you are working with a concept or theory:

- A concept is something abstract, and a theory is a collection of evidence.

- A concept gives a name or label to the idea behind something that does not require testing, like the concept of faith underpinning rituals and ceremonies of a given religion or the reasoning behind a new car design that would benefit customers.

- Theory would be something like there is compelling evidence that the Earth actually orbits the Sun, not vice versa.

- A concept is a general idea that evolves, and a theory is named as the best explanation for an observed phenomenon.

We can have different views of a given concept, but for a theory to hold, we must try to explain it through empirical evidence.

More questions? See questions 19 and 20.

How Does Action Research Fit in Education?

I n 1961, a Brazilian educator and philosopher named Paulo Freire led an action research project in which hundreds of sugarcane workers learned to read and write in just a few months. The Brazilian government recognized the potential of the approach and created a system of *cultural circles* to replicate his approach. These cultural circles brought together elements of literacy with social and political activism.

Action research fits naturally with the field of education. Loosely defined, the field of education encompasses school teachers, school administrators, and the students they serve. All participants can be action researchers. Let's explore an example from the field of education.

A New Third-Grade Teacher. Fatima is a veteran elementary school teacher. This year, she has been asked to move from her fourth-grade class to teach in the third grade. She noticed when she was a fourth-grade teacher that students would arrive to her class at the beginning of the year not knowing their multiplication tables. Typically, by fourth grade, students are expected to have memorized their times tables up to 12×12. This is necessary because in fourth grade, deeper mathematical concepts are explored that require mastery of those facts. Now that Fatima is a third-grade teacher, she has decided to tackle the problem head-on.

She did a quick Web search of how to teach multiplication facts and saw a variety of approaches. She decided that using flash cards seemed to make the most sense to her. They are quick to administer, take little teacher effort, and progress is easy to track. She began with a lesson in which students made their own flash card sets. Each set would have all multiplication facts with a question on one side and answer on the other. She tested all students with a random set of questions drawn from the multiplication facts before starting the intervention, so she had a *baseline*. She decided 30 questions on the *pretest* was enough to find out how much they knew. The test results confirmed that most students had not mastered the facts yet. The average score on the pretest was 22% correct.

Fatima set up a schedule of when each set of facts would be learned. One week the students would practice with their threes, the next their fours, and so on. Every day during the week, first thing in the morning, students would pair up to teach each other with the flashcards for 15 minutes. This is enough time for students to be exposed to each weeks

12 flash cards 10 times. Each week, there would be a test on Friday encompassing all that was learned during that week, and in previous weeks. The tests were cumulative in nature. At the end of 12 weeks, Fatima administered a posttest that was identical to the pretest, so she could see if there was a difference. You'll remember the average score on that pretest was 22%. She was pleased to learn the average score on the same test 12 weeks later was 93%. She decided the intervention worked, and she would do it again in subsequent years. She also decided she might improve the project if she looked at differences between boys and girls in the next year. She suspected some of the boys might not respond to flashcards as well as the girls. But that would be next year's project.

More questions? See questions 14, 15, and 16.

How Does Action Research Fit in the Health Sciences?

I n the health sciences, action research is often referred to as *participatory action research* or sometimes *people-centered health*. However, unlike in business and industry, action research in health care is a fairly new phenomenon. It is most often encountered in nursing. New because in the health sciences, the tradition is to rely on large-scale randomized studies. And so, action research does not fit well with the research tradition in the field. In large-scale medical research, much attention is directed at validity (or more generally threats to the validity of the findings) and generalizability (these findings will be applicable to other settings and other individuals). The notion that small-scale research is only applicable to a particular situation does not fit well with the broader field. In the health science fields, the focus remains on rigorous and technical investigations, whereas action is participant (or patient) centered and focused on small-scale learning and development. This dichotomy in the field is less prevalent in the nations of Europe, but it remains a source of tension, particularly in the United States. Let's explore an example from the field of health sciences.

Do We Need Hospital Support Nurses? Hospital administration is becoming increasingly aware that nursing staff are spending much of their time conducting intake interviews. This time might be better spent on direct patient care. Administration decided to create and administer a hospital-wide survey, to all medical staff, seeking guidance on appropriate steps. While the perceptions of the nursing staff would likely be the most informative, other hospital staff are also stakeholders, for example, doctors, clients, and patients, and may guide better decision making.

Administration was particularly interested in the possibility of hiring several Hospital Support Nurses (HSNs). These new staff positions could directly support the nursing staff in tasks that are not directly related to medical care. The survey posed questions in three general areas: (1) Identify tasks that HSN staff could perform, (2) determine the relative acceptance of this new staffing position, and (3) gain awareness of and better understand other possible solutions.

Once the survey results were compiled, administration shared the results along with an executive report to summarize results. Several open focus group meetings were scheduled to discuss results and make decisions. Hospital administration decided they would conduct a similar follow-up survey on the resulting decision in 6 months.

More questions? See questions 13, 15, and 16.

How Does Action Research Fit in the Behavioral and Social Sciences?

I n the behavioral and social sciences, that is, psychology, sociology, and so on, action research is also called *action learning, evaluation practice,* or sometimes *participatory action research.*

Psychologist Kurt Lewin coined the term action research in the mid-1940s. Lewin contended that action research was a mechanism for social improvement. He viewed action research as a collaborative relationship between participant and researcher, where both find benefit and improvement. This was entirely anti-establishment, but Lewin felt that that in the social sciences, compared to the hard sciences, action research could be conducted with rigor. During World War II, Lewin worked with scholars at the Tavistock Institute of Human Relations that examined the relationship between the science of military personnel selection and the emotional impact of war and incarcerations. Tavistock still maintains a focus of participatory action research in social psychology. Let's explore an example from the social sciences.

A New Patient Survey. In a substance abuse clinic, a group of staff were talking over lunch about how incoming patients had to fill out a lot of paperwork, leading patients to become suspicious that their private personal information was being exposed. A few clients expressed this concern, and others simply would not complete the intake paperwork, thus reducing the numbers of clients potentially served. This was contrary to the clinic's mission of serving all, without question. The staff decided to create a short survey and to attach it to the top of the intake paperwork. It asked four simple questions and looked like this:

You are not required to complete all of this paperwork, but the more complete your responses are, the better we can serve you. Do not include your name on this. It will remain anonymous and private.

1. How comfortable are you providing us with personal information?

2. What recommendation do you have, if any, that can help us make you more comfortable?

3. How confident are you that we can keep your information secure?

4. What recommendation do you have, if any, that can help us secure your personal information?

Initial results cause staff to make several small changes to the paperwork, including better communication about the security of client information. Staff decided to use this survey for a month and then compile data to analyze. Staff then decided to conduct this research every few months, perhaps with little tweaks to improve the survey, to continue to improve the experience of participating clients. This single group action research design was implemented by staff directly for clients that they serve and helped them get back to their mission.

More questions? See questions 13, 14, and 16.

How Does Action Research Fit in Business, Management,and Industry?

Action research fits naturally with business, management, and industry. In business, it is often referred to as *participatory action* research, and less often as *collaborative action research*. In a nutshell, the researcher is participating in the research and collaborating with others to find solutions, not simply consuming results from others. Let's explore an example from industry and business.

Industry and Collaborative Decision Making. At Solar Turbines, a Fortune 500 company owned by Caterpillar, management deployed something they call an Efficiency Board. Solar Turbines designs and builds turbine engines for industry. On this Efficiency Board, any employee can begin a conversation about somewhere they see a possibility for some increased efficiency. Put more plainly, somewhere an employee might see a problem. This is the beginning of the action research process, recognizing an area that needs improvement. The employee writes down and posts a suggestion on the board that is placed prominently on the production floor for all to see. In the case of Solar Turbines, they have a very large facility with varied production buildings dedicated to particular projects, so there is a board in each building. For example, in the machine shop where they craft the actual turbine parts, there is an Efficiency Board. Similarly, in the shipping and receiving facility, there is an Efficiency Board. The board is unlike a simple suggestion box of old; it invites proposed improvement, and the proposal is tracked publicly.

The board looks like a big spreadsheet, each row for an issue and each column to document the progress that issue is making. On the Efficiency Board, the situation is tracked as the issue is explored, from left to right. From the reported potential efficiency, to proposed action, to a data collection plan, a resulting decision, and follow-up data collection to evaluate results. When satisfied, the issue is retired. In this particular example, all stakeholders benefit and do so quickly. The floor worker, the manager, the supervisor, the owner, indeed the shareholders benefit from this approach to dealing with day-to-day issues. Whether the initial suggestion was a good one or was misplaced, the results benefit all. Can a floor employee re-suggest something similar? Of course. This too is a part of action research.

More questions? See questions 13, 14, and 15.

How Can a Gender Theory Approach Impact Action Research?

S imply put, a gender theory approach to research involves the researcher examining the world through the lens that places emphasis on the social construction of gender. And so, a gender theory approach to action research involves the participant researcher using that lens. Gender theory arose in the late 1970s and 1980s to directly challenge the idea that masculinity and femininity arise out of biological differences. Instead, it suggests gender roles were and are constructed by society. This is best evidenced by different gender roles in different cultures around the world. Gender is not individual, but it is influenced by those around us. Parents, siblings, friends, media, and of course, our feelings. Indeed, whereas once one could only choose an identity in their mind and with their behavior, now one can also choose it by altering their body. In universities, this movement led to the replacement of *feminist studies* with gender studies, which focuses on gender identity choice and creation. It isn't simply about male and female; it is about a spectrum of gender and an understanding that we create it.

There is a strong overlap between gender theory and action research. Both challenge traditional thought. Gender theory challenges traditional conceptions of male and female as a dichotomy, and action research challenges the traditional thought that a researcher needs to be outside of the research and not an active participant. Both emphasize the empowerment of individuals, in which people actively engage in decision making and understanding. Both emphasize the development of personal agency as endeavors and choices, and both challenge the establishment.

Some action researchers might focus on gender-relative research questions. For example, an action researcher in a local clinic might ask: Do young women feel welcome in the clinic and are they receiving the services they want? Another action researcher might ask a similar question but use the lens of gender theory: Is the satisfaction with clinic services related to patients' sense of gender identity? At minimum, a gender theory lens calls for the action researcher to ask questions and place findings from an action research project into the context of the influence and impact of gender identity construction.

More questions? See questions 18 and 21.

How Does Critical Race Theory Impact Action Research?

Emancipatory action research is an extension of action research. While it embraces the same participatory nature of the research, it also calls for social change as a result of the research. And so, while traditional action research has the researchers as stakeholders, *emancipatory action research* positions the stakeholders as agents of social change.

Unlike most academic disciplines that espouse to be free of bias merely because they are "academic," critical race theory (CRT) takes an activist approach that seeks not only to understand racialized social structure, but to change it. It is the activist element that naturally aligns with action research. Similar to *emancipatory action research*, CRT assumes that institutional racism exists and through this lens examines existing power structures.

There are three commonly held tenets in CRT. First, racism is ordinary. By definition, racism is systematic and institutionalized discrimination designed to subjugate groups of people based on race (or skin color). Businesses and educational systems are run by a dominant group rooted in White male privilege, leaving racism difficult to address because skin color is often not acknowledged as an issue. It is the very nature of "color blindness" that often prevents communication and change. Second, the fundamental need to gain status through material gain leaves little incentive to address racism. Why would a White male give up power when there is no upside? Third, race is a social construction that the dominant group uses as convenient. There are several examples where this is apparent. Think of colonialism. It is convenient to refer to indigenous peoples as "savages" when natural resources are targets for national wealth. In an action research context, understanding CRT is vital to reflection and action in that its understanding can open dialogue where everyone's voice can be heard.

More questions? See questions 17 and 21.

What Is the Difference Between Exploratory and Confirmatory Action Research?

The approach to creating your action research project comes out of some need. The Action Research Cycle (ARC) begins with the identification of a problem, which leads to creating a research action plan. That plan, which includes a research question and data collection plan, might be exploratory or confirmatory.

Exploratory action research is appropriate with projects when the action researcher is not sure about the variables involved, and how or why they are related. This is most of action research at the start. You may identify some problem but not fully understand the causes or associated variables with the problem, so you explore what you think is involved. It's often conducted before a confirmatory action research project. Let's get more concrete.

Confirmatory action research occurs after several iterations of an exploratory project. It begins when the action researcher has a good or better idea about the causes and effects. The knowledge you take into this confirmatory stage has emerged from an exploratory project you have already done. Consider the following example.

Devonne has been a social worker in an urban center for 12 years. He has constantly been bothered by his inability to improve the condition of the homeless population in the neighborhood. He decides to get more concrete and measure the impact of his efforts. But he does a lot of things and isn't sure which makes or does not make an impact. He recognizes there is literature in the area, but some of strategies the research suggest do not really apply to his particular community or situation.

Phase 1: *Exploratory*. Devonne is known and trusted in his community and decides to develop an interview protocol. He and his team approach a random sample of the homeless population in his community to ask questions about what they see as obstacles to escaping poverty. They also ask what seems to be working well. He and his team decide they will collect data over the period of one week, and then compile and analyze results.

Phase 2: *Confirmatory*. Once the data were considered, the team discovers trends in certain areas concerning what is needed and what is working. They choose one area in particular, the need for temporary shelter, and decide to conduct an action research study documenting the potential benefits of temporary shelters. They record the frequency of use and decide to deploy a similar questionnaire to gauge response. Results inform future work, and they can be more confident they are moving in the right direction.

The nature of the knowledge about a particular problem and potential solutions determines which phase, exploratory or confirmatory, is appropriate. Getting smarter about a problem is almost always a good first step.

More questions? See questions 34, 35, and 36.

What Are the Weaknesses of Action Research?

A ction research encompasses a series of robust methodologies, but as with all approaches to research, there are some real weaknesses to look out for. These issues also exist in traditional research, but perhaps to a greater degree in action research. What weaknesses should you be aware of?

- **Measurement focus.** You can't be confident of your results if you are not sure your measures (e.g., direct observations, tests, surveys, etc.) are accurately measuring what they are supposed to measure. Action researchers may fall prey to this problem more than traditional researchers because the research is less formal and faster. As a result, caution should be exercised when interpreting results. To be safe, you might want to think of your findings as close to accurate, not perfectly accurate.

- **Cultural responsiveness.** Culture is a collective of ethnicity, language, religion, beliefs, and social habits. Action research is certainly well poised to address the intricacies of culture. Its emphasis on research participation ensures that the work is meaningful and well grounded. Additionally, the researcher typically has experience and knowledge of their participant base, which may be diverse in terms of culture. Action researchers need to be particularly careful here, because not all cultures will appreciate the approach to research. For example, some cultures may be rooted in a tradition of the spoken word, and you may have selected an observational or survey design that requires a written product. Still others may face language barriers, creating a rift between the researcher and participant. Even so, the action research paradigm is still more adept at dealing with cultural differences than tradition research.

- **Power dynamics**. Even though action research intends to seek equality and equity at the forefront, it is impossible to have an equal playing field, through either institutional restrictions or systematic structure. Indeed, action research doesn't get done without someone's initiative, commitment, and skill, which by definition change the power dynamics. If power dynamics are not acknowledged, it is possible that your project may take on a patronizing flavor, and participant agency may be demeaned. On the London Subway (the Tube), when a train approaches, a pleasant voice reminds riders to mind the gap between the platform and train. We offer the same advice, *mind the power gap.*

Action research is grounded in social change and has the potential to impact issues of social justice. Good action stems from attending to its strengths, but also its weaknesses.

More questions? See questions 90 and 94.

Social Justice in Action Research

In principle there should be a collective agreement and shared responsibility amongst all those involved in an action research project.
—Gelling and Muinn-Gidding

How Can Action Research Be a Form of Social Justice?

I t is no secret entire groups of people have been systematically marginalized in our society and don't have the same opportunities and privileges as dominant wealthy, White, heterosexual male counterparts. Historically, this was thought to be because people of color or those in poverty did not value the ideals to succeed in the dominant culture. If *they* only worked harder and cared more, *they* would be successful. The pronoun *they* is used intentionally here, as this assimilation model (also known as a deficit perspective) is deeply embedded in our society and is often used to explain disparities of marginalized groups. *Their* problems are *their* fault. Social justice, on the other hand, strives for equality and equity with respect to how wealth, opportunities, and privileges within a society are distributed.

Social justice isn't a new term, but incorporating it into action research is a departure from the typical lens through which we view our practices. Social justice is often referred to as an approach that enables us to critically examine our practice, and it can be used as a lever for us to make changes to systems to more accurately reflect and include society at large.

As it applies to action research, social justice can be achieved when we are concerned with developing an inclusionary system that is committed to meeting the needs of all, regardless of their perceived status. Thus, action research can be a form of social justice through advocacy by explicitly linking issues of practice to wider social implications of those practices. Action research in the name of social justice encompasses *just and honest* investigation, exploring its effects with respect to equity and fairness.

More questions? See question 2.

Why Is Ethics Important in Educational Research and Action Research in Particular?

Three words: *Respect, Beneficence, and Justice*

These three words should be at the forefront for you and any person in the position of serving others before you start any action research project. Here's an example.

Beginning in 1932, in exchange for free health care, the U.S. government infected roughly 600 unknowing African American males with syphilis to study its untreated effects. Once funding for the study was lost in the 1940s, researchers continued the study knowing full well that their test subjects would never be treated, nor would they ever know they were infected. Not until Peter Buxton leaked the Tuskegee experiment to media, and after several congressional hearings, was the experiment terminated in 1972. To be clear, we are not a talking about the 1700s here. This was the disco era. It was about 30 years of some of the most atrocious abuse of human beings in the United States. While there have since been sweeping changes to formal research protocol, and though action research is typically not this controversial, the Tuskegee experiment should still serve as a cautionary tale for anyone who engages in any systematic investigation. So, back to those three words that should guide us:

- **Respect.** First, emphasize human subjects' protection. Minimize potential harm and maximize potential benefits. Though changes and innovations action researchers use are typically done to improve our environment, we should still be sure that we respect human dignity, privacy, and autonomy. We should be open with our participants about our investigation and give them the option to participate, or not. This is particularly important with vulnerable populations (e.g., minors, incarcerated individuals, patients, etc.).

33

- **Beneficence.** Second, try to ensure participants' well-being. We need to consider how the research will benefit the participants in our study, as well as society at large. If we keep good records of our research activities, and avoid careless errors and negligence, our research becomes a form of advocacy that promotes social good and limits social harm.

- **Justice.** Consider and avoid discrimination against participants on the basis of sex, race, ethnicity, or other factors not related to the investigation.

More questions? See questions 25 and 90.

23

Do I Need to Get Some Kind of Approval for My Action Research?

I n general, no you don't need to get approval for action research projects. By definition, action research is a process of critically examining your workplace toward the betterment of those you serve, whether students, patients, or clients. In traditional research in which participants are recruited, there is well-defined process researchers follow to gain approval for their studies. Typically, the research proposal is vetted by an institutional review board (IRB), and a series of questions about the ethics of the study will be addressed. As a ground rule, if what you are doing was going to be done with or without the research component, you do not need to get any external approval.

Having said that, there are some situations where you will want to seek approval for what you are doing. If, for example, you are working with a vulnerable population, the very young or old, the very sick, or those with limited cognitive capacity, it is better to err on the side of caution and seek approval. If no IRB is available, then a workplace superior (perhaps your professor if you are a student) would be someone to consult. Action research projects carried out by undergraduate or graduate students typically require some kind of approval, although it may be expedited. At the very least, letting participants know you are collecting and analyzing their data is fair and can allow participants the opportunity to opt-out.

More questions? See question 28.

What Is Informed Consent, and Why Is It Important?

C onsent can only be given by adults of sound mind. In contrast, assent can be given by others (e.g., children) if they choose to participate, but only with formal consent from an adult guardian. *Informed consent* grew out of the medical field to help preserve patient dignity and privacy. A patient of sound mind should be given the opportunity to fully understand a course of treatment, be given the right to accept or refuse that treatment, and be given the right to share or conceal information that arises as a result of the treatment.

Similarly, informed consent in the context of action research is a participant's right to know what the research is all about, and the right to refuse to participate if desired, without retribution. That is to say, if a student, patient, or client chooses not to participate in the research project, they won't face any kind of retribution as a result. In fact, the default position in any action research project is that the participant does not want to participate unless they say otherwise; hence the idea of consent. Action research projects need to be transparent, easy to understand, and completely optional.

In many fields, often the "intervention" or "treatment" will occur whether or not the participant offers consent. This seems to violate the above described doctrine of informed consent. But remember, data are already being collected about *us* without *our* consent. In the course of our daily life, we interact naturally in different scenarios, and many choose to observe our behavior to make inferences. This might be our shopping habits, driving habits, the TV shows we might be watching, and of course, what websites we visit and what links we click. This is research, but there is no informed consent, and this is par for the field. Because if it was something that was going to happen anyway, researchers do not usually need informed consent, because the action will occur with or without the research component.

An example back in the world of action research might be when a teacher wants to try a new teaching strategy. Perhaps, using flash cards with a kindergarten student to determine if it is an effective way to teach math facts. That is well within the bounds of ethical actions a teacher might take, because it would happen whether or not the teacher chooses to employ an action research design. Even if the teacher would like to analyze those data to see if the flash card strategy worked, we are still on safe ground.

If, however the teacher wishes to share results with others, then we have crossed the line where we might need informed consent. It is very clear that if the research project is specifically designed to share the information with others, then informed consent is needed. And, if some unusual risk is faced by participants, then we are back into the world where informed consent is needed. For example, if a nurse wished to find out if taking patients on daily walks through the hall was effective at improving patient morale, it would require informed consent. The patient might face some risk because they are in a public setting when being exposed to the research action, and they might feel uncomfortable. In this case, the medical practitioner should present the idea to the patient and ask if they are interested in participating in the research project.

In situations that involve participants who are not capable of giving informed consent, for example, young children or those with cognitive impairments who might not understand the potential risks of the research, then a parent or caregiver can give informed consent for the individual.

More questions? See questions 26 and 28.

Who Are the Stakeholders in Action Research, and Why Are They Important?

The primary stakeholder is always the participant, but of course, there is more to the answer. You might, depending on your field, think of a patient, customer, client, or student as a stakeholder. At the end of the day, this is who you work for, and their betterment is why you engage in action research. Truly, anyone affected by the change resulting from your research is a beneficiary—a stakeholder. There is some controversy about the word *stakeholder*, because it might imply a power dynamic or relationship that puts the researcher above the stakeholder. While this can be true in more traditional (outsider) research, in action research, this perceived relationship is not as prevalent. As long as action research is directed at the betterment of practice, there is no conflict or power dynamic. Having knowledge of research methods and deploying that knowledge is purely ethical and actually acts as a way to defend changes to outsiders.

There are three kinds of stakeholders the action researcher should consider when designing a study and thinking about implementing change.

1. **Primary stakeholders.** These are people immediately and directly affected by the action research. For example, if you are changing a classroom practice in an effort to improve outcomes, the student is the primary stakeholder. If you are changing the color of a website to increase traffic to a product, the customer is the primary stakeholder. If you are moving the hospital shift schedule from 11 pm to midnight, the patient is the primary stakeholder.

2. **Interested stakeholders.** These are people not directly affected by the change but are nonetheless interested in the outcome. For example, if you are a third-grade teacher in an elementary school and decided to experiment using math flash cards, other third-grade teachers might be interested stakeholders. The principal of the school might also be an interested stakeholder. And certainly, the parents of the students are interested stakeholders.

3. **Unknowing stakeholders.** These stakeholders are not always obvious. Imagine an action research project where a construction engineer decides to redirect traffic around an underground pipe improvement project. The question might be, should the road be closed in one direction and repair the other side, or should the road be closed altogether and create a detour? In this case, the primary stakeholders are clearly the drivers that use that road, and the interested stakeholders are those charged with road improvement in the city. The unknowing stakeholders might be the residents of nearby neighborhoods who are impacted by the detour or change in traffic pattern. And perhaps the birds who live in the trees that grow next to the road improvement project. Even the trees are unknowing stakeholders!

More questions? See question 10.

Why Is It Important to Strive for Confidentiality and Anonymity?

It's rarely possible to have complete confidentiality or anonymity in action research, partly due to the communal nature of the work, but also because participants are active in the process and have perspectives or experiences that are valued as part of that process. Everyone knows exactly where everyone stands. Confidentiality or anonymity is particularly difficult for qualitative approaches to action research. That said, there are some safeguards that get us closer.

When done, it's especially important to share your findings with participants, but take care if findings are intended to be shared with others. For example, data might be collected in the normal course of our work, and it makes sense to calculate mean scores for our own comparisons and evaluation, but sharing those scores with parents is problematic, particularly if you disaggregate your data by characteristics of interest, for example, by gender. Discussing confidentiality and purpose from the beginning and throughout is part of informed consent and helps to build trust among participants.

During an action research project, clean the data. When possible, you will want to remove identifying characteristics, like name, ethnicity, illness, and so on, before conducting analyses (unless they are a part of the analysis). And keep the data secure. Be sure to password protect them, and house them in a secure location, preferably not on the same machine used to analyze data.

After the project, think long and hard about who is going to see and or use the end results. In a classic example, there may only be one or two students in any given school that share a particular characteristic of interest, for example, receiving special education services, and to report those scores could identify certain students and violate anonymity and/or confidentiality. This is why schools restrict score reports to having more than five students in a sample. This concept also holds true in health sciences with rarer forms of illness. Maybe there was only one case of a given illness at a hospital that year. When results are going to be shared, if there is any way a single participant can be identified, you have broken participant confidentiality.

Should I Treat Children in Action Research Differently Than Adults?

Yes! Involving minors or children in research raises unique ethical dilemmas. The unique risk is well documented in traditional research, and there are protocols in place over the world in an effort to not bring harm to vulnerable participants during any research endeavor. However, these protocols do not adequately address an action research framework where the researcher is devoted to making a tangible and meaningful difference in the lives under her or his care. For example, if a researcher wants to implement a mental health intervention with minors, unintended consequences may hinder social acceptance or have negative changes in home life interactions. When conducting action research with minors, it's critical to keep the following principles in mind:

- First and foremost, care for people in your research. Take time, smile, be kind—all the kindergarten sandbox stuff about getting along with people. The participants in your study are not simply numbers; they are young people with complex lives.

- Even young participants can be a part of the action research. Invite them to be a part of your action research, not just subjects. Depending on how young, this participation will look different. The key question to ask yourself is, will everyone come out of the study, researcher and participant alike, better off?

Many of you, especially students, will have single action research project you are required to conduct. For your own sake, treat action research as something more. It is a way of thinking about being logical, but also empathetic. Whether working with individuals or a community, you will garner far more respect (and better results) if you keep your ear to the ground and you heart involved. *Live action research for your life, not the day.*

More questions? See questions 22, 23, and 24.

What Does a Sample Consent Letter Look Like?

D epending on your circumstances, this letter may or may not need to be edited. The gist of the letter is what is important.

Date

Dear (consent giver),

This year, I am taking a course through (xxx) University to earn a (xxx) degree in (xxx). An important part of my work this year is completing an *action research* project. Action research is a way of examining one's own actions and investigating how those actions can influence others. My project is to examine (xxx). I would be appreciative if you would

- (choose to participate) *or*

- (grant your permission for your child to participate).

My data collection methods will include (xxx). I guarantee confidentiality of information and promise that no names will be made public. Names will be replaced by coded numbers that will make participants unidentifiable. Participation is easy and will

- (not involve any stress or risks) *or*

- (involve minimal risk, like [xxxx])

If you choose not to participate, there is no consequence, so feel free to ignore this request if you want. If you choose to participate, and you wish to be kept informed about the progress of the research, I can keep you updated via (email or phone or address).

If you consent, I would appreciate it if you would sign and return your permission at your earliest convenience.

- I, _____, as parent/guardian of _____
  _____, consent for my child to participate in the
  action research project described above. I understand that at any
  time I may withdraw my consent.

or

- I, _____, consent to participate in the action
  research project described above. I understand that at any time I
  may withdraw my consent.

Please include your contact information if you want to be updated during
the action research project.

More questions? question See 22.

Research in Your Field

4

*The positive mind . . . asks how phenomena
arise and what course they take, it collects
facts and is ready to submit to facts,
it subjects thinking to the continuous
control of "objective facts."*

—Lezsek Kolakowski

What's a Literature Review, and Do I Need One?

A literature review is an examination and synthesis of other studies related to your action research topic. Typically, a literature review is a lengthy document that details what is currently known in the area, and how that body of knowledge is related to your research question. A literature synthesis is usually the first step in academic dissertation work for master's or doctoral students. It is a necessary step for students, because before they begin to write a meaningful question to investigate, they would first want to know what others have done, where there is agreement among scholars, and most importantly, where there is disagreement or inconsistency in the field.

In an action research project, this endeavor is a bit overboard. After all, the whole idea is that the action research project emerges out of practice, not out of an extensive literature review. However, there are some aspects that might serve an action researcher as well. After all, someone may have already looked at your research question. Granted, it may be in an unrelated context, but similar studies can alert you to what not to do, or what to watch out for.

An action researcher should at least *skim* the literature. Most studies have an associated abstract that describes in brief what was asked and answered in the study. While access to full articles is often difficult or impossible without expense, abstracts, in contrast, are free to read. Using the powerful Google Scholar tool (scholar.google.com), an action researcher can easily gain access to abstracts, so a quick literature skim is more doable. If you discover an article that is highly related, you might try to read it—maybe from your university library (most are open the to the public). In addition, look at the articles that cite it (also available in Google Scholar), because they are likely similar. Performing this simple literature skim gives you better insight into what others have done and can help guide your question and study.

More questions? See questions 32 and 88.

What Are the Steps in Doing an Efficient Literature Review or Synthesis?

If you do find yourself in need of a literature review or synthesis, as many students do, there are steps you can follow to make it less painful:

1. Have a clear and well-thought-out research question before starting. This helps you to better organize your time. If you start with an ambiguous question, you will needlessly spend time looking for irrelevant studies. You may still change your question.

2. Assemble a set of keywords related to the research question and use them when searching. As mentioned, Google Scholar is your go-to search for related literature, but there are other search tools that are available, especially if you have access to a university library.

3. When closely aligned research articles are found, look closely at the reference sections of those papers and follow up on related studies. In Google Scholar with the click of a button, you can link to articles that cite that article of interest, too. So, in effect, you can look into the past and the future once you find an article of interest.

4. When reading through abstracts, take note of findings and decide whether or not your research question needs some adjustment. Keep in mind as you do this, you are getting smarter about the topic, and change may be warranted.

5. Think when reading related literature. What findings seem the same? What findings seem different? What are the variables of interest, or in other words, on what does it *depend*? This is important in helping you shape your action research project.

Thinking of this process can help you save time, something we all value in our busy lives. The key is to be efficient with your action research project. Clear questions, good keywords and phrases, looking at related studies, thinking critically about that question again, and looking for relationships between studies related to your question are an excellent start.

More questions? See questions 29 and 32.

Should I Read Action Research Articles?

A ction researchers like you probably know what a research article is, but you may not know that scholarly articles typically follow a standard format. Knowing this can help you quickly look through the text to find exactly what you're are looking for, for example, theory, design, and analysis. Simply put, a research or scholarly article is a manuscript, online or in print, that shares a research project or study. After the abstract (or brief summary), research projects usually present a brief literature review in an *introduction*, then the procedure or *method* of the research, the *results*, and a *discussion* about the importance of the study and how it fits (or doesn't fit) with other studies. This is affectionately referred to as IMRD. Commit this to memory.

When a research study has been completed and the story written, it can be submitted to a journal for publication. The acceptance rate for publishing varies depending on the quality of the journal. The best journals accept a low proportion of the studies submitted, perhaps less than 10%. Most lie somewhere between 10% and 50%. Less reputable journals accept more than 50% of the studies submitted to them. The least reputable journals accept 100% of submissions and may even charge the author to publish. This kind of journal is becoming more common with the advent of online publishing. It takes very little technical expertise to set up a phony journal to collect money from would-be authors. Critically think about your sources!

Reputable journals engage in a process of peer review to evaluate the quality of the work. When a submission is made, the manuscript is sent to two or three reviewers who are experts in the field, who provide comment and an evaluative decision on whether or not the manuscript is worthy of publication. Perhaps they will decide it should be rejected, or perhaps they will decide that with some revisions, it can be resubmitted for re-evaluation. On rare occasions, a manuscript will be accepted outright.

Understanding the publishing process will help in two ways. It can help you to know how and where to publish your work, but it can also help you understand how rigorous journal reviews help to ensure the quality of published research is high, and hence trustworthy.

More questions? See questions 92 and 98.

How Do I Evaluate the Articles I Find?

When you look at and consume research literature, you want to start by isolating the research question. This can usually be found in the abstract or early on in the introduction. In an action research project, you don't want to or need to consume all related literature, so, you need to be adept at quickly perusing the article to find the research question and then, of course, the answer.

It is beyond the scope of this text to provide you with the training to fully understand the pros and cons of different research methods. Instead, you will need to rely upon the peer review process that journals use to evaluate the quality of that method. Simply put, if the article is published in a reputable journal, then you can rest assured that it has been well vetted, and the results are likely sound.

We mentioned that research articles generally have four sections: an introduction, a description of the research methods, a presentation of the results, and a discussion of those results (IMRD). Depending on your proclivity, you might gravitate to one of these sections. The abstract should give you much of the information you want, but sometimes, you need to dig a little deeper to understand the background to the research (introduction), the design of the study (method), the nuances of the findings (results), and the author's opinion of those results (discussion). These four sections form the core sections of any research article, whether action or traditional research.

More questions? See questions 31, 92, and 98.

How Do I Plan for My Action Research Project Before I Start?

Thinking through your project before you start requires both creativity and critical thinking. In terms of creativity, the action researcher begins by noticing a problem or issue. The way to address the problem or issue will be different for different people. While there may be similar ideas from different people who experience the same problem, no two proposed solutions will be the same. And this is appropriate. The way to address a problem depends on the context and requires novel and creative thinking to understanding intricacies. Much like having and raising a child. There is no one way to do it, *because it depends.*

In terms of critical thinking, a flow chart can make sense. It need not adhere to the rules of flowcharts, just a simple diagram of the process. Critical thinking involves questioning and an openness to multiple solutions. Further, it demands that the action researcher be able to describe why decisions were made, and why not other alternatives. Looking back and questioning decisions is both fundamental to critical thinking, but also to action research. In Figure 33.1, you can see an example of a project that was planned on cocktail napkin. This is a real flowchart of the research project, and was subsequently published.

In this project, we started with a pool of 12 teachers and assigned each of them and their classroom of students to receive some training or not. In this case, it was teaching critical thinking through literature. The two groups of teachers then gave reading, writing, and thinking tests to their students. Over a 2-month period, each group was taught as usual; however, the teachers that received training added components to foster critical thinking. That group received some classroom observations to understand to what degree the new strategies were being used. Finally, in the last rectangle, you can see a series of comparable post-tests were given. The question as to whether the teacher training initiative led to student improvement could be answered, at least in this context. Classic action research.

Of importance, the classroom observation led to our ability to revise the training. Some teachers did not fully understand the intricacies of the strategies. In subsequent trainings this was addressed, and we did it all again. Better classic action research.

More questions? See question 7.

Figure 33.1

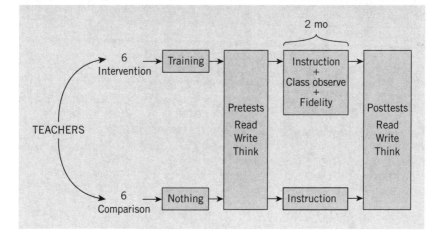

Moving Your Research Forward

5

Rather than following generalized predetermined standards, decisions about rigor should be based on the specific organizational context, information needs for the evaluation, and anticipated benefits and costs of available methodological alternatives.

—Marc Braverman and Marie Arnold

How Do I Narrow Down My Topic?

You'll remember that Luke and Todd wrote this book. This is a Luke and Todd story. We often notice our students (we are both professors) are off-task more than we would like during our team-taught classroom lectures. Because there are several causes and behaviors that make up off-task behavior, we just can't find a single solution. We need to have a plan to narrow this topic down.

- **Reflect**. Action research is conducted within a given context, and we need to consider our own context when defining a problem. What do we see? What do we want to change? How do we measure it? In the above example, we see off-task behavior during lectures, and we want to minimize the behavior. Students chatting, students on their phones, students shopping online. However, upon further reflection we believe that Todd's lectures are the culprit, and the function of the students' behavior is that they are bored and confused. Ah. Luke might be onto something, but again we can't just look up "How does Todd give a good lecture?" and fix the issue. We need to narrow that down so we can focus on our research.

- **Be specific**. Replace or add one or two words to be as precise as possible. We might want to replace "good" with "effective elements." In this case, the purpose was to increase "engagement" or more specifically "on-task" behavior. Now we're getting somewhere. We are going to solve that Todd problem.

- **Discover the research question**. Continuing with the example, "What are elements of an effective lecture to increase on-task behavior?" Now we can conduct a focused literature review based on a defined independent variable, elements of an effective lecture, and a measurable dependent variable, on-task behavior.

Narrowing the topic is actually a pretty important step. It is the stage where you really have to think about what you are asking.

More questions? See questions 36 and 37.

How Do I Make Sure My Research Is Rigorous?

Action research project results may be disseminated to many different audiences, including other practitioners, experts, external organizations, and so on. Whatever the group, each will interpret the results for their own purpose, for example, funding decisions, employee evaluations, industry improvement, and so on, and each will ask the question, can I believe the findings?

Technically, this is a validity question, or more precisely, the accuracy and trustworthiness of methodology, measures, findings, and interpretations. Given the reputation of action research over time, it really comes down to perceptions of research rigor.

Remember that action research is an iterative process that requires reflection and adjustment on a regular basis. For action research to be rigorous, you need to be flexible throughout the process. In other words, you need to adjust your designs, variables, data collection, analyses, and interpretations based on previous findings. This could be considered a research program or agenda, but what distinguishes action research from traditional research is that these changes are specific to an individual/local issue that requires the researcher to participate in the process, not merely an objective observer. Thus, your decisions may change according to your specific needs and not necessarily generalize to a greater population. That said, here's how to make your action research project rigorous.

Commit to using an Action Research Cycle (ARC) approach, realistically and regularly. Typically, for the first iteration of the cycle you observe a particular phenomenon, reflect on what you want to change, ask questions, and design projects to address a given issue. Often, this is more of an exploration into the issue that confirms it really exists. The second part of the cycle addresses methodological issues in an attempt to change or improve the issue, and finally a third part is an evaluation of the previous two. Basically, sustained replication is key here to (re)assure our audience that our claims are well grounded.

Collect good data. Of course, this hinges on having a good research question. Data collected can be quantitative, qualitative, or a mix of both depending on the question. For example, if you want to improve hospice care, you might want to collect interview and observational data along with some direct observation of practice. Triangulation is the key here. When all data are put together, results point to an answer to your question.

Check your work to defend your claims. This sounds rather simplistic, but in practice, it's much more difficult to do. Think time and resources. However, this is a critical component to increasing internal validity and rigor. For example, perspectives often vary in qualitative approaches, as would be expected. To address this, check your interpretations and tentative conclusions with your research group before, during, and after each cycle.

More questions? See questions 29, 30, and 31.

What Do Good Action Research Questions Look Like?

You have narrowed down your topic by identifying an issue that needs addressing, brainstormed potential causes and solutions, and you might even have a general idea of how you will go about studying it. But how do you develop a good question? This is a critically important step. Follow five steps. The question needs to be:

1. **Important and focused**. It directly addresses the problem and will result in a benefit for your participants.

2. **Manageable**. It can't be too broad like "How can I get people to pay attention?"

3. **Contextual**. You don't want to completely redo or make wholesale changes to your work that would increase workload. Rather, you should focus on what can change within the normal scope of work to improve the situation for all stakeholders.

4. **Open-ended**. You don't want to ask yes/no questions like "Does incentivizing my salesforce increase sales?" A yes/no question does not provide enough information to continually improve. In other words, once the question is answered, there is nowhere else to go. With action research, you want to have a variety of potential answers that provide you with flexibility moving forward. It may not just be incentivizing. It may be that different kinds of incentives work differentially depending on context and individual wants and needs. A good starting prompt begins with How, or Why, or What. Something like "What kinds of incentives will increase sales?" is a good start.

5. **Reflective**. Can you reflect on the findings? What do the data say about your sales force? And what do they say about my practice as a manager? In the above question, you will get a variety of answers to help guide decisions.

More questions? See question 44.

37

What Is the Difference Between Qualitative and Quantitative Approaches to Action Research Design?

Once you have identified a focus and question, you can think about your approach to research design. In simple terms, approaches are divided into purely quantitative, purely qualitative, and mixed. The research design is a function of the approach and the question. A qualitative researcher is interested in figuring out why things are the way they are—to describe cultures, groups, or events—often a microscopic perspective. A quantitative researcher is interested in relationships—and how they might be generalized—a wider perspective.

Like in politics, people usually fall into one camp or the other. Or at least they lean one way or another. There are a few generalizations that might help us better understand the distinction and contrasting ideas, which isn't always this clear cut.

Traditional research projects you come across will likely lean more one way than the other. More recently there has been interest in mixed approaches, like action research. Research combining both perspectives provides a fuller understanding of issues and problems in practice.

Qualitative Approach	Quantitative Approach
Context specific	Seeks to generalize
Asks how and why	Describes what
Subjective understanding	Focus on objective understanding
Descriptive and observational	Numerical, measured, and statistical

More questions? See questions 38, 39, 40, and 41.

What Are Common Qualitative Research Designs in Action Research?

In qualitative research, the goal is to better understand deeply with intense and/or prolonged contact in a given situation. We often interpret as we go and keep questions open so we don't miss new insights or emerging themes that could lead to discovery. Qualitative designs are situated in contexts that can provide a thick, rich description that allows the researcher, as an instrument, to look at phenomena as a whole, rather than trying to parse out individual components, like quantitative research approaches. Below are common qualitative research designs action researchers use.

The goal of a *case study* is to learn about phenomena of interest by studying a particular instance. Cases are selected purposively by investigating extreme, typical, or contrasting cases. Case studies typically involve long-term involvement. For example, you may want to learn about spending habits of teenagers, so you track your child's expenditures for a period of time to look for patterns.

The goal of a *document analysis* is to learn about phenomena or events that happened in the past by exhaustively studying old documents, interviewing people instrumental in the event, and so on in an effort to capture the full range of perspectives on a given issue.

The goal of an *ethnography* is to understand a culture, broadly defined; how the lived experiences of people in a particular group interact to form a phenomenon that can be studied. Ethnographies use an insider (emic) perspective that is particularly useful for the researcher. In an ethnography, it is critical to question motives/biases. For example, a teacher wants to understand cultural differences between students. Because you "live" in the same classroom context, you document your observations to come up with a theory about those differences.

More questions? See questions 40 and 41.

39

What Are Common Quantitative Research Designs in Action Research?

In quantitative research design, you need to identify the target variables. In other words, choose your intervention and the outcomes you are hoping to improve. There is also a need to determine how to investigate the relationship between the variables, and control for outside sources of error. Below are some quantitative designs action researchers commonly use.

A *single measure* design is typically used when implementing ideas. You try something and measure what happens. This design is weak because there is no starting point, but it is often your only choice. Your research design might look like this:

Do something to one group, then collect data.

In a *single-subject* design you are typically working with a small group. Baseline data are collected to establish behavior prior to some change you are going to make. Subsequent data indicate behavior under different changes you make. For a small group of people, maybe three to five, your research design might look like this:

Do nothing, then collect data (baseline).

Do something, then collect data.

Do something different, then collect data.

Do nothing again, then collect data.

More questions? See questions 40 and 41.

QUESTION

40

What Are Some Better Quantitative Action Research Designs?

A simple *pretest/posttest* uses a single group of people. In this design, there is a known starting point that makes it easier to determine effectiveness, or change, but it doesn't control for group variability. Your research design might look like this:

Collect data.

Do something to one group.

Collect data again.

The *non-equivalent control group* design typically compares two intact (non-random) groups. Of course, randomizing is a better choice, but we almost always can't do that (nor would we really want to in action research). Because of the non-random nature of the groups, it's important that the groups can be comparable on variables of concern so that differences arise from what we do, not group or measurement variability. Although there is the potential issue of pretest scores influencing posttest scores (memorizing answers), this is a superior design to those described thus far.

Group A.

Collect data, do something, then collect data.

Group B.

Collect data, do something different, then collect data again.

More questions? See questions 39 and 41.

What Are Some Common Mixed-Method Action Research Designs?

As one would surmise, a mixed-method approach to action research is exactly what it says. It is a project that uses both qualitative and quantitative approaches in a given project. Again, the question drives the type of research tradition chosen.

Traditionally, action research has been more closely aligned with qualitative research. However, because we often have quantitative data, we can leverage both qualitative and quantitative approaches to address our practical (local) issue *and* add to the body of knowledge in a rigorous way. There are three basic ways to look at mixed-method designs.

- **Quantitative first approach.** Analyze data you already have before you act. For example, you may already collect numbers on something you've done (teachers have quiz scores, nurses have vitals, managers have sales figures). Using those numbers can help form your action research project.

- **Qualitative first approach.** Another approach might be to conduct an action research project that is qualitative in nature, and then decide that you want to collect numerical data after analysis. This is the more classic action research approach.

- **Same-time approach.** Perhaps in your project, you decide to conduct interviews and focus groups to answer our question. Your interview can have closed-scale questions (quantitative) based in numbers and can also feature open-ended questions in which participants have the ability to provide free responses to prompts.

There are trade-offs, of course. Qualitative research is time and resource consuming but is close to the ground and is personal. Quantitative research can seem detached but can also be fast and efficient in terms of time and resources. Blending the best of both, mixed method, might be a way to bridge the differences.

More questions? See questions 38, 39, 40, and 43.

Can a Program Evaluation Also Be Action Research?

N ot typically. You know that action research is a systematic process where an individual participates in investigating an issue of interest. Action researchers not only conduct the research but have a vested interest in the outcomes because it affects their daily life.

Program evaluation, on the other hand, is a systematic process that investigates effectiveness of enacted policies or programs, often by outside researchers. While individuals have a vested interest in the outcomes, decisions are often made from higher up in the food chain, not at the individual level. A few things to remember about the differences between action and program evaluation:

1. Action research intends to improve one's professional practice. Program evaluation intends to improve a program based on findings.

2. Action research helps an individual understand a practical problem to help guide future action to address the practical problem. Program evaluation evaluates the relative effectiveness of a program by comparing a program's stated goals with associated activities on specified outcomes.

3. Action research uses both qualitative and quantitative research approaches that are appropriate to an individual's context. Program evaluation uses more "rigorous" research approaches that are often externally designed and conducted.

4. Action research focuses on understanding a problem and an associated intervention to address the problem. Program evaluation focuses on effectiveness at a grander level.

5. Action research could be conducted without an intervention. It could be just gaining a better understanding of one's context. Program evaluation wouldn't exist without an established program in place.

How Do I Choose My Action Research Design?

In earlier questions, we discussed identifying a problem, finding a focus, reviewing the relevant literature, and writing research questions. Let's put it all together now, with an example from a teacher.

Luke noticed that his students weren't reading at grade level, and he wanted to change that. He reviewed some related studies and noted that there was some evidence to indicate that using simplified text might help. The research question is, how would simplified text affect reading comprehension? Sounds pretty solid and doable within the scope of my own work. So, how do I actually do an action research project?

Our research question drives our research design. Before I get started, I have to ask some pragmatic questions.

1. What does my participant sample look like?

2. If it matters, what is the demographic makeup of my participants?

3. How large is my sample? (number of participants)?

4. How long should the intervention be? Days? Weeks? Months?

5. Do related studies seem to match with what I think is reasonable?

6. What is the best way to collect my data?

7. What are the measures I'm going to use to assess reading?

8. What is the timing of my data collection?

9. How often am I going to test my students?

I have a fairly homogeneous group with respect to demographics and evenly split between gender. I decided that the book that I'm going to teach will take about 2 weeks, and similar studies support this timing. I'm going to use the same quizzes I typically use, which means I'll test students before, during, and after reading the book. This question points me toward a quantitative approach. Now, let's head into Part 6 to really dig deeper into the methods of action research.

More questions? See question 34.

Research Designs and Methods

The first and most important condition for differentiating among the various research strategies is to identify the type of research question being asked.

—Robert K. Yin

What Are Referents, and Which Work Best With Action Research?

C ompared to what? When you engage in action research, this is a question you should be asking yourself. Decisions based on data involve comparison to bring meaning to your project. There are three decision-making referents: normative, criterion, and individual. Without a planned referent, it is difficult to interpret data collected. Collecting data alone will not answer a question; you will need to choose one or more referents.

• *Normative referents* are comparisons between our participants/ subjects and what might be considered normal in the larger population. Sometimes these are called "norms." For example, if I take an IQ test and score 100, it doesn't mean I answered 100 questions right. My score is compared to a large pool of people who are representative of the entire population—the norm reference. In most IQ tests, a score of 100 means I scored about the same as the average of that larger population. These normative referents are very common across disciplines.

• *Criterion referents,* in contrast, do not compare data or scores to a larger population. You can think of a criterion referent as a line in the sand. It is a predetermined level to which you can make a comparison. For example, a business might set a target growth rate of 2% for the year. At the end of that year, the comparison of interest is whether or not the business succeeded. Establishing a criterion to which you will compare data is an area of interest in many fields of study.

• *Individual referents* are perhaps the most valuable, because you are comparing people to themselves. For example, imagine the patient enters a hospital in the emergency room. A series of diagnostic measures are first taken—pulse, weight, temperature, and so on. That same patient who is later admitted to the hospital will continue to have the diagnostic measures administered. Perhaps temperature every few hours and weight every day. The data collected are used to gauge the recovery rate of the patient. Compared to their first body temperature, which may have been high, has the patient progressed toward normal body temperature? Using an individual referent, is most meaningful when the person is the only case you are examining. Of course, tracking the temperature of a patient over time gives you an indication of relative progress toward wellness, but keep in mind that the goal temperature of 98.6 is in fact a normative referent.

Although not always a perfect fit, comparing results to normative, criterion, and individual referents gives our decisions perspective.

More questions? See questions 36, 45, and 62.

How Do I Randomly Choose My Participants?

D etermining who will participate and how you choose them is critical to the success of your action research project. This is known as a sampling plan, and its purpose is to generalize to a greater population. Action researchers aren't typically concerned with generalizing to a greater, or target, population, but it is still useful to know the various approaches, so you can choose the most appropriate one for your setting.

The four approaches here generate, to varying degrees, random samples. Random sampling helps to assure you that groups (if you are using a multi-group design) are comparable. These are also called *probability samples* and are presented in order of the rigor of the random sampling design.

- **Simple random.** Select participants so that everyone has an equal and independent chance of being selected. Choose the population and flip a coin. This is typically done in observational research, because between-group differences theoretically wash out.

- **Stratified random.** A target population is defined by characteristics of interest, for example, race/ethnicity, gender, age. Then participants are randomly assigned to experimental conditions following protocols of simple randomization. This is a strong approach, because it can better assure the researcher that all groups are represented in the sample. This is especially important when there are very small groups of people with unique characteristics of interest.

- **Cluster.** Intact groups are chosen based on sharing characteristics of the targeted population. For example, you might select a cluster of hospitals or schools all serving urban areas, if that was your area of interest. Once you have clusters, you choose to randomly select participants.

- **Systematic.** Every *n*th participant from the target population is assigned to a group and may dictate an over- or under-representation of the sample. This sampling plan works well with action research.

More questions? See questions 44 and 46.

How Do I Not Randomly Choose My Participants?

There are many approaches to selecting (sampling) your participants. While selecting random samples is a common and appropriate approach in traditional and quantitative research, non-random approaches are more commonly used in qualitative and action research. The nine non-random approaches, also called *non-probability* samples, are presented in alphabetical order. No one is more rigorous than another; they are simply more or less appropriate in different contexts.

- **Concept creation**. Participants are chosen because they can help the researcher generate concept or theoretical understanding. This is clearly appropriate if you are in a concept building phase before you begin your research.

- **Convenience.** Whoever walks in off the street gets chosen. Think getting paid to do a survey when going to the mall. This isn't the greatest sampling plan, because it's hard to know who will end up in your study.

- **Critical**. Participants are chosen based on being at the extreme of a "typical" group. For example, in the field of education, a teacher action researcher might want to sample all students with autism.

- **Maximal variation.** Participants are chosen based on how different they are on a given characteristic. Think healthy versus unhealthy people. In this sampling plan, it is critical to define the characteristic. For example, what defines healthy? Once the characteristic is defined, participants can be compared on how much they differ on that characteristic and selected appropriately.

- **Opportunistic**. Participants are chosen mid-study because new information is necessary to answer your research question. For example, if you find that your chosen participants don't have the knowledge required to answer your research question, you might choose to find more participants. This is not a recommended approach, because it creates significant threats to internal validity. A better approach would be to start over.

- **Purposive.** Participants are chosen for a particular reason. Think fourth graders. They are in a particular classroom at a particular time because the school schedule dictates it. They are usually in the school because it's in the same neighborhood where they live. Neither of these is happenstance. This is the most typical sampling plan in action research. You are interested in a particular group and purposefully select them.

- **Quota.** Participants are chosen by a particular characteristic. This sounds similar to stratified random sampling, but here once a quota of participants is reached, no more data are collected from that particular strata. Data continue to be collected until each quota is reached.

- **Snowball.** Participants are chosen based on referrals from other participants. When the topic is pretty complex or unfamiliar, it is pretty common to call in a participant would have that knowledge. It is different from opportunistic in that the sampling plan is selected before data collection starts. It's an internal validity thing. Perhaps a social worker wants to interview undocumented immigrants. The action researcher may choose a snowball sampling plan. She knows three or four who are her friends, then she asks them for referrals to others, and so on.

- **Typical.** Participants are targeted chosen based on how they represent a particular group according to an outsider. Think about a small business hiring a marketing agency to provide them with a list of a particular demographic group. Maybe the small business is interested in a particular age group, with a particular salary range, in a few particular zip codes. This is a common approach, and at some point, you have probably been in one of the groups and contacted as a result.

More questions? See questions 44 and 45.

How Do I Create Groups?

Before you can understand grouping, let's first review sampling. The idea of sampling or finding a small group of people for your study arises out of the notion that you typically can't access an entire population. It is within that sample you will be creating groups.

Grouping participants is very important in action research, and those groups typically emerge from your research question. For example, a math teacher might ask, "If I expose second-grade students to flash cards two times a week, will they improve their basic multiplication math knowledge?" Clearly the primary sample will be second graders in the teacher's class. However, the action researcher might also want to add a second group of second-grade students from another class, who do not receive the flashcard intervention. In this case, you have two naturally occurring groups—one called the treatment (flash cards) and one called the control (no flash cards), and you can compare the average scores of each group after the data are compiled.

The research question might also drive you to establish different groups. In the example above, perhaps you are interested in knowing if girls and boys responded the same way to the flash card intervention. In that case, you have added a grouping variable, depicted below.

	Female Group	Male Group	Overall
Flash card group	mean score girls, with flash cards	mean score boys, with flash cards	average score, with flash cards
No flash card group	mean score girls, no flash cards	mean score boys, no flash cards	average score, no flash cards

This new grouping variable allows you to dig much deeper into the question, and you can imagine there are other ways to dig deeper.

More questions? See questions 62 and 73.

What Is a Case Study?

A case study, simply put, is a research project in which there's a single case being examined. This is a natural fit with action research where context is of paramount importance. This approach is common in the social sciences and industry. The research strategy is also used in traditional research, but is often shunned as unscientific. Traditional research seeks to generalize knowledge from research, whereas action research is concerned with practical solutions in context. In the field of education, the case might be a student, the principal, or a school. In the health sciences, this might be the patient, the staff, or the hospital. In industry, this might be the client or customer, coworkers, or the business at large. The key is there is a single entity you will examine. The entity or case of interest can vary depending on your research question.

Even in case study research, it is still important to collect multiple data points to triangulate. For example, an action researcher might want to examine the behavior of a good school principal. To triangulate the research, the researcher might want to interview and observe the principal, interview teachers, interview students, examine the school website, and send a survey home to parents.

There are a few different philosophical approaches to case study research, and scholars argue about the merits of each. In general, case study researchers do not come from a positivist perspective, but instead see research as more open-ended. They approach case study from the perspective that the researcher can't control or place bounds on the case being studied. In contrast, a constructivist approach treats the case as something that can be studied subject to constraints or boundaries. The positivist perspective might fit better with action research because it relies more directly on observation in a natural setting, and not heavily on literature and theory building. But, as mentioned, scholars argue about the merits of each perspective.

More questions? See question 64.

QUESTION

49

When and How Would I Use Interviews?

Interviews are verbal interactions between two people with the intent of collecting relevant qualitative data regarding a single participant's experience. To do this, you need a series of questions.

Interviews are appropriate when a closer interaction with participants is needed or wanted. For example, simple observation of a patient to determine level of satisfaction seems inadequate. And perhaps a survey seems insensitive. Why not ask the patient a few questions?

Interviews are particularly appropriate when you might not have a large group of people you are studying. Large groups make interviews difficult, because they are time-consuming and can yield vast amounts of data (words, in this case).

Individual interviews, and their sister, the focus group, are often analyzed with large-scale software. NVivo is the most popular and powerful. Coding responses by hand is an option if your sample size is very small. You will be looking for trends in the responses from your participants to help you make decisions and answer your research question.

More questions? See questions 50 and 51.

In General, What Are the Different Kinds of Interviews?

There are three types of interview questions.

- *Structured* interview questions are also known as standardized, patterned, planned, and formal. They are a series of predetermined questions given in the same order to different people. All responses are compared to each other on a given scoring guide, scale, or rubric. Structured interviews are typically used in a commercial setting where candidates can be compared objectively and fairly. This is particularly important in equitable hiring decisions, but not always applicable to action research.

- *Semistructured* interview questions are also known moderate, hybrid, and combined. As one would surmise, semistructured interviews contain a small set of predetermined general topical questions asked to multiple participants but allow for probing questions as they arise. The probing questions allow for more of a spontaneous conversation. This is particularly germane to action research in that it allows the interviewer to get at the heart of the matter if the participant needs prodding.

- *Unstructured* interview questions are also known as informal, casual, and free-flowing. Unstructured interviews are exactly that. There are no pre-planned questions. The interviewer brings up a topic to the participant, and they go from there. Given the time commitment of interviewing, unstructured interviews are not typically used in action research, because the interviewer is investigating a particular phenomenon, and unstructured interviews may not yield on-topic responses.

More questions? See questions 49 and 51.

How Do I Write Interview Questions and Interpret the Answers?

O nce you have chosen your type of interview questions, you need to write them. Whichever type you choose, you will typically follow similar protocols.

Develop and write down important questions directly related to the variables of interest, driven by your research question. Be sure to be focused, but flexible. Try to avoid "shut-down" questions like "why did you . . . " or yes/no questions. These put the participant on the defensive and do not usually yield opportunity for follow-up. Don't be afraid to (respectfully) ask for greater depth of explanations. Develop conversation starters to facilitate conversation and deeper understanding and plan for potential probing questions to respond during participant conversation. Starters like "Tell me about . . . " and "Help me understand . . . " are not judgmental and put the participant at ease.

Print out and bring questions to the interview. It helps keep all parties on task and helps with transcription or note-taking.

Once you have transcriptions or notes, you need to make sense of all this information. Be sure to interpret as you go. Keeping questions open so you don't miss new insights that lead to discovery and being open to emerging themes allows you to look at the phenomenon as a whole rather than trying to parse out individual components. Here's how to make sense of all the words.

1. **Take good notes**. It's OK to paraphrase and to use your own personal shorthand but be consistent and be sure that you got it right. This is where a recording can help.

2. **Read your notes**. As you read your notes, write down themes that you see. Or use computer software to help.

3. **Cluster your themes**. Ask yourself, how do these themes fit together, and how to they relate to my research question?

4. **Interpret your findings**. Did you find any surprises? Were there any potential misunderstandings? What do the results say? Did some things appear more than others? Did some not appear at all?

More questions? See questions 49 and 50.

Why Would I Use Focus Groups?

U se interviews when you want to get information on a small number of participants. However, the more interviewees one has, the more time it will take. A focus group, on the other hand, is a group of people gathered together. They can interact with each other in a guided discussion on a particular topic in a nonthreatening environment. Typically, focus groups are used to give market researchers feedback or guidance on a given product or service. The focus group might be given lunch afterward. Broadcast media companies use focus groups to gauge group reaction to new productions. Hollywood uses focus groups to test different movie endings with different groups.

Action researchers use focus groups, which allows them to get similar qualitative information from multiple participants in one setting. For example, you might not have time to interview all beer-drinking people about their preferences. You can more easily get them all in the same room, at the same time, maybe a bar, and ask the same interview questions.

In addition to saving time and legwork, there are other advantages. First, participant interaction is dynamic and typically more thoughtful when compared to quick responses in a survey. Second, focus groups are flexible by design. The interviewer (called a moderator) knows what the direction of the discussion should be but has the latitude to change direction if participant interaction warrants it. Participants possess a body of knowledge that when combined with others' can take the focus (pardon the play on words) into a different and potentially more meaningful direction than was intended. Group interaction and participation are very important.

More questions? See question 53.

How Do I Conduct Focus Groups?

N ow that you have assembled a focus group, what kind of things do you need to keep in mind? At the forefront, social dynamics. The relationship between focus group members can impact outcomes. For example, when conducting a focus group at a workplace, some employees may be more outspoken and better known than others, which can diminish full group participation. Similarly, in a school setting having teachers and principals in the same group may diminish responses because of a power relationship. Teachers may fear retribution if they speak their mind. In general, having more participants in the same focus groups can create a safer place and reduce potential "noise" from socially derived responses.

A few things to attend to when you are deciding to use focus groups. First, focus groups can't give us information at an individual level. All questions are designed, and ensuing discussions are aggregated to the group level. Second, there is typically no pre- or post-focus group. Focus groups cannot tell us how things have changed over time. Third, because focus groups are by definition representative of a group of interest, outcomes cannot be assumed to generalize or represent a broader population.

Remember, quality outcomes depend on group interaction and discussion. If participants feel intimidated or distracted, they are less likely to be forthright and honest. Try to find a place where participants feel welcomed. Comfort is key. Try to foster relationships and ensure as much equal participation as possible. The action researcher who can do this can get robust findings that will point to, and support (triangulate) decisions for an appropriate action plan.

More questions? See question 52.

How Do Ethnographic Data Collection Methods Support Action Research?

An ethnography is a qualitative research approach that examines people's interactions in their natural settings in which the researcher is immersed, a participant observer. This differs from other research approaches where an observer does not interact with the participants and fits well within the action research tradition. Ethnographic methods look at people's words and actions, both explicit and implicit, in an effort to create a narrative account of a given cultural environment within a theoretical framework. It has been called *deep hanging out*.

Ethnographies are typically conducted by anthropologists but can be very useful in action research because the researcher is already living in the culture under investigation. This is important because the researcher is not only walking a mile in the participants' shoes, but knows the dialect, shares meaning, and has already developed a comprehensive understanding of the environment over extended time and experience.

Of course, like any other action research approach, there are research parameters to collecting rich and meaningful ethnographic data. First, the actual process of collecting data is iterative and reflexive. In other words, the researcher observes then reflects on the phenomenon to build and support a theory. The action researcher then continues to test that theory in practice over time. This is typically referred to as grounded theory.

Testing theory multiple times is critical to internal validity given the subjectivity of the researcher as the actual instrument. Triangulating observations with key interviews is useful, because a single method is typically unreliable. Another way to triangulate is to have informal conversations, similar to an unstructured interview. One of the great advantages of ethnography is that almost everything you can get your hands on can be considered data.

More questions? See questions 38 and 72.

Can You Tell Me What I Need to Know About Surveys?

How do you feel about surveys? Are they fun or exciting? Do you like doing them? Or are they annoying and a poor use of your time? Sometimes it depends on the survey. Have you ever run into a survey and started it only to give up because it doesn't make sense? You need to be careful about how you design your surveys and survey questions if you want results to be valid.

A survey is a measurement instrument that collects data; it might be a questionnaire or an interview. Surveys can be *cross-sectional*, a moment in time (the "snapshot"), or *longitudinal*, perceptions over time. And within longitudinal surveys you might look at trends that follow a topic over time or examine cohorts or panels, to follow a group or small sample over time.

Surveys are either *sample* based or *census*. With census you are examining an entire population. For example, the U.S. government has a census every 10 years. They contact everyone. In contrast, most surveys take a sample of the population. This is usually done because trying to contact the whole population is difficult and expensive.

Now, if you want to generalize to a broader population, you will need to randomly select the sample, or alternatively, systematically select a sample that looks just like the population. For example, let's say you want to know what people think are the most important factors keeping them from quitting school. You probably can't take a census approach, but a sample is doable. You might be able to randomly select students from all over the country, or maybe just locally. An alternative approach is to skip random sampling and never generalize. This is the more common approach in action research. You can survey the people of interest, directly, and ignore issues related to generalizability.

More questions? See question 49.

How Do I Write Good Survey Questions?

What would seem to be a very straightforward procedure may be more difficult than you think. Despite best efforts, you will probably write survey questions that raise more questions than answers. There are no real hard and fast rules about how to write perfect questions, but rather a set of guidelines. Common sense is the real rule. There are five common problems you might run into, which are easy to understand and avoid. By way of example, we are going to show you what some problematic questions look like.

Although the system of education in California is of good quality, it really should not be mirrored in other states. Agree or disagree?

In this case, you may agree the California system is good and should be mirrored in other states, but that response is not an option here. In this case, some people won't know how to respond, and may not. Others will not know how to respond but will respond anyway. This kind of problem is called a *double-barreled* question. Be careful to avoid questions that have multiple ideas or phrases. Be watchful for words like *and*, *or*, and *but*, because they are often indicators of a double-barreled question.

Did you spend a lot of time studying for your degree?

We don't really know what "a lot" means, and it is bound to be different for different people. Maybe the respondent thinks 1 hour is a lot, and someone else thinks 6 hours is a lot. A better question might simply ask, how much time do you spend studying? We refer to this problem as *ambiguous wording*. Make sure to be concrete with questions, and do not leave them open to different interpretation.

On average, how much time do you prepare for class each week?

    (a) *Less than 1 hour*

    (b) *Between 1 and 2 hours*

    (c) *Between 2 and 4 hours*

    (d) *More than 4 hours*

We have all seen questions like this. But why not simply ask for an estimate of time? How many hours? You can always come back later to apply the constraints to interpret your data if you ask an open-ended question. We call this problem *constraining the metric*.

Do representatives in government contribute to its corruption?

This is a *leading question*. Its premise is that the government is corrupt. And the respondent can agree or disagree about what people think but cannot question whether or not the government is corrupt.

Do you love your children?

Very few will say no. This kind of sensitive question may not get an honest answer. Who would tell you they don't love their children? We call this problem *social desirability*. If an answer is more socially desirable, people will gravitate to that answer, whether true or not.

Try to avoid these trouble spots: double-barreled questions, those that have ambiguous wording, those that constrain the metric, those that are leading, and those that are prone to answers that are rooted in social desirability. And remember, common sense is the guiding rule.

More questions? See questions 51 and 55.

Can I Use Direct Observations in Action Research?

Yes! Observations are typically divided into two categories, *participant* and *nonparticipant*. Participant observations are more commonly used in action research. Participant observation happens when the action researcher engages in and simultaneously experiences the environment, for example, as both a customer and retail clerk at a mobile phone retail outlet. As a customer, the participant observer lives the experience and feels emotions of buying a mobile phone. This experience, in turn, helps to shape their service approach when back at work.

Direct observation is an important data collection tool and can be a critical component of action research for a couple of practical reasons. First, as you can imagine, if the action researcher is involved in the process, then they would be in a good position to document the *what* of a process and situation that outsiders might not have. Second, observations can yield data about the context. Again, an action researcher who participates in the experience can also better identify *why* something may be happening. Whether your observations are overt (everyone knows that you're doing them) or covert (you do it on the sly), when triangulated with other forms of qualitative or quantitative data, observations can serve as powerful explanations. We suggest you conduct observations whenever you can.

More questions? See questions 39, 40, 41, and 58.

What Are the Elements of Conducting Effective Observations?

1. Collect as much contextual information as you can about the situation you are in. Even if information seems trivial, write it down. You will probably forget it later. Using a personal journal is a good way to go about doing this. You can document a lot of environmental variables before anyone is present simply by taking photos with your phone. You can always revise and redo your analysis, but you can't go back in time to collect more data.

2. Focus on the question(s) you want to answer to help define the path of your observation. The behaviors of interest are what you are looking for. If they are very specific, consider using a checklist. A simple way to add to your data collection is to take observations every 5 minutes (interval observations), checking off boxes about what you are seeing. For example, if you are conducting an observation in a classroom, you can have a checklist of a dozen variables of interest, and you can simply indicate if you saw it every 5 minutes.

3. Be aware of your biases and work to minimize them. Observations clearly raise issues of subjectivity, but if constructs and associated behaviors are defined clearly, potential bias is minimized. One way to do this is by cross-checking your data. You could have a person use your protocol alongside you to see if you both are seeing the same thing. This is an excellent internal validity strategy.

More questions? See question 57.

How Do Interval Observations Enrich Action Research?

M any researchers will observe an environment and check off whether something occurred or did not. Or perhaps they might also describe what happened. A more fruitful way of gathering data is though *interval observations*.

An interval observation protocol calls for the action researcher to decide first what behaviors to observe and second how often to observe them. Let's explore an example to make this idea clearer.

A kindergarten teacher is concerned about classroom behavior. He decides to systematically collect data to better understand the scope of the problem. A colleague will come into the class and count the number of times certain behaviors occur. Instead of simply counting over the whole day, the colleague will take a count for each 30 minutes. A short version of the checklist might look like this.

	9–9:30	9:30–10	10–10:30	...
disruptive to class	4	3	1	
talking out of turn	6	4	1	
out of seat	7	3	2	
...				

Judging by the data collected, it appears most poor behavior occurs at the start of the day. A planned action, thus, might want to address that time of day in particular. Another observation can follow after some intervention (the action) has taken place. The strength of the approach is in documenting times of day the behaviors are likely to occur.

Similarly, an engineer might use the same approach studying traffic patterns in a problem intersection. It is one thing to know a lot of people are turning left during the day, and quite another to understand what times of day it is happening most or least. This kind of information leads to the potential for better solutions to traffic problems. There are several variants of this observational approach. The one factor they all have in common is the added dimension of time.

More questions? See questions 57 and 58.

What Are Experimental Designs, and Are They Practical in Action Research?

In a "true" or experimental design, participants are randomly assigned to treatment group(s) or control group(s). A "true" experimental design is very difficult to do in action research, because you will typically use a sample of convenience, the people you are working with. Randomization is great in research if you can do it. Imagine you have an experiment with two conditions: (a) the pill you developed and (b) a placebo, a pill that looks and tastes the same but is some inert compound. When you randomly assign participants to each group, you are virtually assured, if you have a large sample size, that the groups will be comparable in all ways. An easy way to think if this might be if you had a thousand people and randomly assigned them to two groups, you'll get close to 250 males and 250 females in each group. Other attributes would distribute the same way, so you can assume that the groups are the same in all ways, except for which pill they get. Any differences after the experiment can thus be attributed to the pill.

A quasi-experiment design randomly assigns groups to conditions instead of people. Not ideal, but far more practical in the real world.

More questions? See questions 61 and 75.

What Are Quasi-experimental Designs, and Where Do They Fit In?

With a quasi-experimental research design, you assign groups to different conditions in your action research study, randomly. This is unlike experimental designs in which you randomly assign people to conditions. There are three main types of quasi-experimental designs. The types below are listed in ascending order with respect to rigor.

- **Descriptive.** This is more or less the first stage of science, and it is pretty much the way it sounds. It attempts to describe a particular situation. Although it can be quantitative, no relationships, comparisons, or predictions are made in this design. Measures in a descriptive design are typically more qualitative and use observations, case studies, interviews, and surveys/questionnaires.

- **Correlational.** A correlational design is a quantitative design that seeks to establish patterns between participants on two or more variables. A Pearson-product moment correlation (r) is the typical statistic. Not only do you notice the descriptive properties (as above), but you explore if variables are related. As one goes up, does another? As one goes up, does another go down? The classic correlational study demonstrates that foot size is correlated to knowledge. Yes, the bigger the foot, the smarter the person. But slow down and think about it. Babies have small feet and adults have big ones, so of course there is a positive correlation. The point here is that bigger feet don't create smarter people, it is just statistically related. *Correlation does not imply causation.*

- **Causal comparison.** Like a correlational study, a causal-comparative design seeks to identify relationships among variables. However, a causal-comparative design attempts to determine causes or consequences of a given intervention between groups. Our research question would need to be, do bigger feet *cause* higher intelligence, not as with the previous example, are bigger feet *related* to intelligence. There are a number of statistical procedures used to determine causality, most rooted in regression analysis.

More questions? See question 60.

Can You Tell Me More About Action Research Designs That Use Groups?

G roup designs are a pretty standard action research practice. In middle and highs schools, teachers usually have more than one section of a given class, so they have a built-in participant sample that fits with group design. A teacher might have three or four different groups of students for the same class, but at different times. In other areas, like marketing, group design also fits well. You can, for example, compare participants by age group or by gender, or some other variable of interest that makes sense.

By definition, in group design, participants are divided into two or more groups. Often one group receives something (the treatment) and other doesn't (the control). There are two basic types of group design in action research, between-groups and matched pairs.

The classic randomized *between-groups design* is when you have two or more existing groups, where either participants or groups are randomly assigned to conditions, and you use a standard pretest/posttest design. Participants are assigned to a particular group, given an identical pretest, given the intervention (or nothing if they are the control group), and then tested with an identical posttest.

Because of the nature of the sample, sometimes you might choose a *matched pairs* design. In this design participants are matched based on certain characteristics of interest, for example, gender, age, interests, and then assigned to groups. There is no randomization. If you can strategically match two groups to be comparable or equivalent on variables that you think might impact the study, you can be more certain that your group design results in valid findings.

More questions? See questions 47 and 73.

Do I Collect Data Once or a Bunch of Times?

I f it's feasible, the most rigorous way to conduct an action research project is to collect data multiple times, or longitudinally, to see change over time. If you want to understand developmental stages, it's important to know where, when, and why they happen.

Collecting data over time can be broken into two broad categories: cross-sectional and longitudinal. Both types are observational. The researcher collects data on participants without manipulating the context.

Cross-sectional designs answer questions about different groups of people on the same variable of interest. For example, let's say your variable of interest is alcohol consumption. Basically, you record alcohol consumption of participants at a same time-point and compare results, then repeat with different cohorts/groups at a later date. In a more visual sense, this cross-sectional design looks like this:

Single point in time observation		
Time 1	Time 2	Time 3
Group 1: Male	Group 1: Male	Group 1: Male
Group 2: Female	Group 2: Female	Group 2: Female

In this example, there were two groups at Time 1, 2, and 3. The groups contain different people, but the underlying assumption is that these groups are comparable, so measurement over time is valid. There may be more grouping or "blocking" variables, depending on your research questions, for example, five different age groups or four different income levels. The defining feature of a cross-sectional design is that you can compare within the time point and over time with different people.

Longitudinal designs (sometimes called *time-series*) answer questions about the same people on the same measure. For example, you may want to know if decreasing alcohol consumption decreases blood pressure in males. In longitudinal studies, you can look at changes over time for a targeted group or even down to the individual level. This is useful because you can go beyond a snapshot to see a sequence of events. For example, you can track alcohol consumption over time for females and males to determine if changes in stress levels affect an increase or decrease in alcohol consumption. As patterns emerge, you can look to other research designs to determine causality. In a more visual sense, this longitudinal design looks like this:

Single group longitudinal design			
Observation female	Time 1	Time 2	Time 3 . . .
Observation male	Time 1	Time 2	Time 3 . . .

There are a few things to keep in mind when considering a longitudinal design. First, because the researcher is collecting *a lot* of data, it is particularly important to be focused on maintaining data integrity. It is easy to lose track of data when a lot of time passes during the study. Second, the researcher will need to monitor participant attrition or addition. Mobility is particularly concerning in schools, which means participants will drop out of the study. Although patients move as well, records are usually accessible with permission.

More questions? See questions 39 and 40.

Are Single-Case and Single-Subject Designs Different?

Yes! *Single-case* design relies on an individual referent, or in other words, collecting data about someone or something, then comparing them to the same person or thing over time. In single-case research design, you are asking and answering questions about a single case. It might be a person, an organization, or an industry. Researchers describe a case study as a sample size of one ($n = 1$). For example, you might be interested in a single Web user's clicking habits when on social media. The researcher is not interested in average behavior across many users, but simply one user. This piece of data might be used to deliver more targeted advertising, to help determine if that user's clicking behavior could be shaped. Not to shape the behavior of all, but to shape the behavior of the individual. In general, findings from single-case design research are not generalizable to the larger population.

In contrast, in *single-subject* research design (often confused with single-case design), the researcher uses a small sample of participants to collect data and collates the data to generalize to a larger population. This is a particularly useful technique when a large sample of participants cannot be obtained. That is true in the field of education with students from low-incidence disabilities (e.g., students on the autism spectrum who are also gifted) or in the medical field with patients with low-incidence diseases. These are situations when the researcher cannot obtain a large group of participants for research, but where legitimate questions still need to be answered.

In single-subject design, the researcher requires a minimum of 3 participants and 9 total data points. For example, you could collect observations on 3 people over time. Then you can compare each person to themselves at 3 data points, and each person to the other 2 participants, giving a total of 9 comparison points.

Unfortunately, researchers in the field of single-subject design have been increasingly calling their methodology single-case design. Very confusing for all. What matters most is that you understand the nature of the methodologies, not what it might currently be called. Richard Feynman, noted physicist, expressed much the same idea—it is not important to know the name of the bird, but instead understand its behavior and nature.

More questions? See question 48.

I Wrote My Question and Chose My Design. What Kind of Data Do I Need?

Action researchers want their decisions to be based on as much high-quality data as possible. The data are used to justify sometimes very important decisions that affect the researcher, the participants, and interested stakeholders. For these reasons, you need to, to the best of your ability, ensure the reliability and validity of your data.

Data that are reliable mean that they are consistently collected and of high quality. This gives you confidence in the accuracy of the data. Your decisions are valid when you make inferences based on reliable data. What you report, after your project, needs to align with what you learned. The best way to ensure both is to gather data from multiple sources by multiple methods (triangulation) and to use group data analysis and decision making. Of course, this isn't always possible, especially in small-scale action research projects.

When the time for data collection comes, there are a couple guidelines you can follow to make it most efficient.

• **Start with what you have.** Pick the low-hanging fruit first: What data are easiest to get? Often there are data lying around that you can use. They may be used to confirm that an issue or problem you suspected exists, and less commonly to answer your research question. In education, you have grades, attendance reports, behavior reports, and so on. In health care you have the vitals collected on all patients and large-scale disease tracking resources (think Centers for Disease Control). In industry, you have very fine-level data about rates of employment and unemployment, wages, price trends, and so on. Our point is, look around for what might already be there. If nothing more, it will inform your research.

• **Collect only what you need.** If you do need to move to data collection, and this will be true for most, be very clear about what data you will need, and for the sake of efficiency (sanity) collect them in the simplest way possible. Take time to make sure your data collection plan aligns with your research question and plan, and that the impending data analysis will indeed help to improve outcomes.

More questions? See questions 66, 68, 69, and 70.

Collecting and Analyzing Data

*An approximate answer to the right problem
is worth a good deal more than an exact
answer to an approximate problem.*

—John Tukey

How Are Descriptive and Inferential Statistics Different?

S tatistics can be confusing. On the one hand, polling or demographic numbers are often thought of as *statistics*, and on the other, some consider analytic procedures conducted on those numbers to be statistics. In other words, numerical values reported are statistics, but the class you might take in university is also called statistics. In essence, quantitative data are gathered and organized, and from that you create statistics to help understand the data. Once you do understand, you can decide if you want to use them. Statistics come in two forms, descriptive and inferential.

- *Descriptive statistics* are what they sound like; they describe the data, and they are used in everyday life, like Earned Run Average, average life expectancy, and average salary. The key here is average (or arithmetic mean), but that's not all. Descriptive statistics also include the spread of scores (range), middle point (median), the most frequent score (mode), and how far a score is from the mean (standard deviation). Descriptive statistics allow you to ask the question, How did participants do? They are also called *measures of central tendency.*

- *Inferential statistics* make inferences from results of the sample generalized to a larger population. In addition to answering descriptive questions, they allow you to ask the question, if the difference was statistically significant, or perhaps if the finding was just due to chance. Inferential statistics are more complicated and may not be as useful in action research, because you're not usually attempting to generalize, although you could if needed.

Even though action research has been more closely aligned with qualitative research, even if you don't use inferential statistics, descriptive statistics can help you triangulate your data to paint the most comprehensive picture so you can make the best decisions possible.

What Is Visual Data Analysis?

Visual data analysis, also known as data visualization, requires that the researcher create plots and graphs of data to draw inferences from patterns. The technique takes large amounts of data and distils them into a more digestible and easier to understand modality. This is an ideal technique for the action researcher because it is quick and easy to do in any available spreadsheet software (e.g., Excel, Numbers, Calc).

Consider a two-variable dataset containing 100 people. For each person, you have a score for happiness (0–100) and a score for wealth (0–100). The boxplot and bar graph presented in Figure 67.1 depict the data.

Figure 67.1

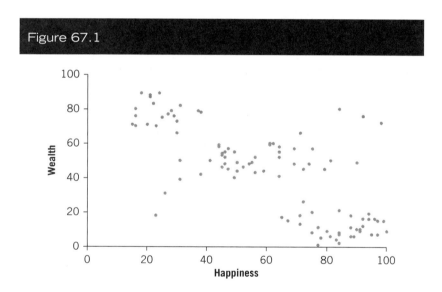

Without sophisticated data analysis, a trend becomes evident. If you were to draw a line of best fit through the data points, it would be sloping downward, from left to right. The clusters of data help to envision this trend. So, in this case, it appears the less wealth you have, the happier you are. Scatterplots are ideal when you are dealing with two variables. Other plots you might want to explore are the box and whisker, the histogram, and the standard bar chart. All provide insight into large datasets.

More questions? See question 84.

What Does It Mean to Triangulate My Data?

In previous questions, we've discussed different ways to collect practical and meaningful data. Triangulation allows for different perspectives using multiple methods or data. Each result or perspective is verified with the purpose of converging on the truth with more confidence. Most importantly, relying on a single data source doesn't paint the entire picture, and because reality is not fixed, it cannot be measured entirely in a positivist approach. Triangulation yields more accurate information when results of each measure converge on the same answer. Essentially, having multiple data sources increases the validity of your decisions.

In technical terms, the reasons for triangulation are (a) enrichment (results add value from different angles); (b) refutation (results are different from common perceptions); (c) confirmation (results support common perceptions); and (d) explanation (results shed light on unexpected findings). Triangulation also minimizes bias. There are three main types of bias:

1. **Measurement bias**. Single data collection techniques provide a single interpretation. Triangulation allows for us to combine results to get a clearer picture. Think about how a single focus group might be biased.

2. **Sampling bias**. The sample is not representative of the target population. Again, results from a single focus group may not represent the population that you want to reach.

3. **Procedural bias**. This stems from pressure on participants to give socially desirable responses. When you use different methods of collecting data, you can get a better sense of the accuracy of answers from different contexts.

In practical terms, you do this already in your day-to-day lives. When faced with everyday decisions, you might ask a few friends for their opinion, maybe a family member, perhaps an expert, and more commonly Google.

More questions? See question 74.

What's the Big Deal About Reliability?

W e often confuse reliability and validity. To be clear, reliability is the consistency and accuracy of a given result. It answers the question, If you use this measure again and again, will you get the same results? Think electronic timing for the 100-meter dash. Validity, on the other hand, is how well the measure actually measures what is says it measures. A given instrument can be reliable without being valid. Olympic electronic timing in sprints is very reliable but is not a valid measure of reading skill. However, and more importantly, an unreliable instrument can never be valid.

There are three main types of measurement-reliability you should be concerned with in action research, test-retest, alternate forms, and interrater.

1. **Test-retest**. The same test is given over multiple times to the same participants. For example, the same vocabulary test is given twice to some third graders, and correlations are calculated to estimate reliability. The standard for test-retest reliability is approximately $r > 0.8$ for group decisions and $r > 0.9$ for individual and high-stakes decisions.

2. **Parallel/alternate forms**. Different versions of a test purporting to measure the same thing can be given to the same participants. You would expect the scores on each test to be about the same (assuming they are on the same scaling metric). Reliability estimation protocols and standards are the same as test-retest.

3. **Interrater**. The degree to which different judges agree on their decisions. Having two raters assessing the same participant work is a good example. Reliability is calculated by percentage of exact agreement. Usually, 85% is the standard.

More questions? See questions 45 and 71.

What's the Big Deal About Validity?

I f someone provides you with a test of mathematics, it should measure mathematics only. If some of the test is in written English, then it is also measuring English language comprehension. Validity is the degree to which a measurement instrument (be it a test, interview, focus group, etc.) measures what it purports to measure. There are several ways of measuring validity of a given instrument:

- **Content validity**. The content of the instrument aligns with the content criteria of the subject area. So, for example, if you wanted to give a test of fourth-grade math, you wouldn't just give a test of algebra. You would also need to include subject matter from the whole year: algebra, fractions, basic functions, and geometry.

- **Criterion-related validity**. The result of a given measurement instrument in a content area should be similar to a different instrument that is measuring the same content area. For example, two IQ tests from different companies should come up with similar or near the same results.

- **Construct validity**. A construct is an idea in your mind. Love is a construct, and you have constructed an idea of what it is in your mind. Because it is a construct, people may have different ideas of what constitutes love. Reading is also a construct. Constructs represent the way we understand ideas, and we usually communicate them with words. Construct validity refers to the degree to which your study, or action research project, is aligned with the construct of interest.

There are quantitative measures of many aspects of validity, but what is most important for you is to understand and be aware of these three major elements.

Validity in qualitative research refers to the degree to which the measures, procedures, and resulting data fit with the research objectives. Five guiding questions can help determine the validity of a qualitative study:

- Does the research question align with the measured outcome?
- Is the research method likely to lead to an answer to the research question?
- Is the data collection method targeting the sample of interest?
- Is the data analysis appropriate?
- Are the conclusions valid for the context of the research?

More questions? See questions 69 and 71.

Why Do I Need to Care About Internal Validity?

U p until now, and particularly in the past few questions, we discussed ways to make an action research project rigorous. This has everything to do with internal validity. It's called internal validity because it's internal to the study. It speaks to the quality of the study conducted. To increase internal validity, you can rule out factors other than the intervention or action as possible causes of change in the outcome. In other words, internal validity looks at the ability to make decisions with confidence. In contrast, external validity is about the quality of the study that relates to generalizability. This is not a big concern in action research. Generally speaking, there is one primary way to increase your internal validity: controlling group variance.

Make the groups as similar on everything as possible, leaving only the intervention or action as the difference. For example, you may want to test your idea that cold weather causes colds. You might define cold weather as exposure to temperatures less than freezing for more than 4 hours per day for 5 consecutive days. Let's say you could design a study with a (treatment or action) group that gets the cold temperatures and a (control) group that gets room temperature. Now, you want to make sure that the action is the only difference between the groups. You will want to minimize any other differences; for example, one group shouldn't have comfier chairs, or get more sunlight, or have more hot baths.

More questions? See question 70.

What Kind of Threats to Internal Validity Are Common in Action Research?

As an action researcher, you face a series of threats to internal validity that can cause you to make decisions that are based on poor research results. Some are more threatening than others, so we'll just give you the top five.

- **History**. External, non-controllable events may occur that influence your observed effects. Maybe something big happened in the news that was related to your study.

- **Maturation**. These are participant changes that can influence the observed effects. This is most often seen with younger participants where there is a large difference in development levels and growth rates, both physically and mentally.

- **Testing**. Your pretest may influence results on the post-test. This usually happens when the study is too short, and participants could have memorized the answers from the pretest. Some might be good at memorizing, and some not. A good solution for this is to use different but comparable measurement tools.

- **Statistical regression**. It is natural when giving any measure that participants will tend to score closer to the mean on subsequent tests. Participants who scored below average on the pretest have a better chance of scoring higher on the post-test, and those who scored higher than the average on the pre-test have a better chance of scoring lower on the post-test. This is simply a statistical truth. Not much you can do about it.

- **Attrition/mortality**. Participants differentially drop out of the study. We hope there is no real mortality. It's just what it's called. This happens in high-mobility areas. Note it and move on.

More questions? See questions 70 and 71.

What Are Blocking Variables?

In a previous question, we talked about sampling and grouping people to answer an action research question. The example we provided looked into whether or not flash cards helped second graders with basic math facts. We also decided to code whether the students were boys or girls, so we determine if there was a differential effect based on gender. That second data point, gender, is called a blocking variable. The first variable was whether they got the intervention or not, and that was fully under our control. The second, gender, was not. We cannot assign gender to people! Can you think of another variable we might be interested in, but that cannot be controlled?

In most fields these blocking variables are the same: gender, race, ethnicity, age, and so on. These are variables you cannot change. There are some blocking variables that are more discipline specific. In medicine, the fact that a person has a disease or not is not under your control, so it is blocking variable. In fact, it can only be a blocking variable, because it would be unethical to give people diseases to study them. In business, the fact that a person is above or below the poverty line is typically not under your control, and so it too is a blocking variable.

Blocking variables are key pieces of data to collect, because they do not take much effort but can yield a lot information. They are the low-hanging, but critical, fruit of action research.

More questions? See question 47.

What Are Ordinal, Interval, and Categorical Data Types, and Which Works Best With Action Research?

Variables you include in your research can be described as ordinal, interval, or categorical (nominal). These are data types. You may have no control of the data type, but understanding them will help you to better comprehend how to later analyze the data.

Ordinal variables are those that occur in a natural order. Perhaps you are collecting data from customers to better target them with specific products. You might be able to collect their income level in four categories: low income (less than $25,000), middle income ($25,000 to $75,000), high income ($75,000 to 150,000), and ultra-high income (greater than $150,000). These variables occur in a natural order, but the gap between each level is not the same. The difference between low and middle income is not nearly the same as the gap between high income and ultra-high income. This is a key characteristic of ordinal variables—they occur in a natural order but the levels, or space, between each may not be the same. It is a questionable practice to use ordinal data with descriptive statistics, like averages.

Interval variables, in contrast, have the same characteristics and an ordinal variable, except the space between variables is always the same. For example, let's say you collected height information from a classroom of fifth-grade students. You would end up with a distribution of data, the heights of all students, that might vary substantially. You might have a student who is 136 cm tall and one who is 156 cm, and an array of students in between. You can sort the students from shortest to tallest on a scale in order of height. And, because each cm is exactly the same, you have an interval variable. In the case based on income level in the previous paragraph, if you instead asked for a specific dollar amount from participants, you would have transformed the data from ordinal to interval scale, because the dollar variable is the same. $10 is $5 more than $5. $20 is $5 more than $15. Each and every dollar is the same. You can comfortably use descriptive statistics with interval data.

Categorical variables (also called *nominal variables*) have two or more levels, but no specific order. For example, if you also collected race/ethnicity information from a customer, patient, or student, they cannot be intrinsically ordered: White, Black, Pacific Islander, Native American, and so on. No one ethnicity is above or below another. These are categories only. Other examples of categorical variables might be eye color, tree species, and gender.

You are probably wondering why this matters in action research. To put it plainly, it matters because it determines what kind of data analysis you can do. Knowing what might be possible before engaging in the action research project allows you to understand what kind of answers you can produce. If you collect data on eye color, you cannot compute the average color, but you can produce a table with the frequency of eye colors. Consider this survey question:

I am happy with this product.

❏ strongly agree
❏ agree
❏ disagree
❏ strongly disagree

You might give each of these categories a value from 1 to 4, and you could calculate an average "satisfaction" from a customer pool. However, because you don't know if the gap between each level is the same, you probably shouldn't calculate an average. This particular question would generate data on an ordinal scale. Often survey scales are used this way, and this is problematic. It isn't terrible. And you might want to assume that these variables are indeed interval. Just understand that is *only* an assumption.

More questions? See question 47.

Does Generalizability Matter in Action Research?

Generalizability refers to the degree to which your findings (results and conclusions) from your research can inform others. For example, if a researcher discovered that giving someone a glass of milk helps them to think more clearly, does that mean it will make others similarly think more clearly? Can the finding be generalized to others? Results from action research may or may not be generalizable, and it is typically not the focus.

In order for the research to be generalizable, certain conditions must be met. The degree to which the conditions are met speaks to the level of generalizability.

The gold standard in research is a randomized control group design. In this research design, participants are assigned to one of two groups. In one group, they receive the *treatment* condition. The other group does not; they serve as a *control*. Of particular importance, the participants are randomly assigned to each group. Every participant has the same chance of ending up in the treatment or control group. For example, let's assume you want to test the idea that milk leads to more clear thinking. You can gather a group of people from around the nation and randomly assign them to the milk everyday (treatment) and no milk (control) groups. You then follow each group and measure clarity of thinking (however that might be done) after a few weeks. Because participants were randomly assigned to groups, you can assume that on average they are about the same on any other variables that might affect the outcome. If you recruited 100 people for the milk study and randomly assigned them to two groups, there is an equal likelihood that each group would contain the same number of male and female participants, 50/50. There would also be an equal distribution of people who like and don't like milk in each group. This is the fundamental reason why randomization in traditional research is key.

The focus of action research is on informing your practice, and so generalizability, while certainly desirable, is not important. You want to understand through informed inquiry what is true about your group, not necessarily how it might apply to others.

More questions? See questions 66 and 93.

Turning Data Into Information

It is a capital mistake to theorize before one has data.

—Sherlock Holmes

Now I Have All These Data. What Is the Best Way to Present My Results?

S haring your project and your results can be an important reflective time for you. Students of action research will be asked to do this in class. Practitioners may be asked to share, or elect to share, at a meeting with stakeholders. No matter the reason, there are guidelines you can follow to make the task easier.

1. *Tell the story of why.* What was the importance to the study? What did you notice that made you wonder or made you want to improve some outcome?

2. *Tell the story of how.* You chose an approach to study. Why did you choose that method over others? What are the intricacies of the method that will help others understand the procedural components of conducting action research? This is particularly important to share, because you can model good techniques, which also speaks to the rigor of the project.

3. *Share results.* To be clear, you will want to share summarized results, not individual results (unless that is appropriate). This has everything to do with confidentiality and protecting participants' rights.

4. *Draw some pictures.* Use data displays: tables and figures (graphs, photos, maps, and charts) to help others draw conclusions on their own, or show how you came up with your conclusions. This might be a good time to discuss some potential weaknesses, because people can learn from your mistakes. Don't be afraid. This is a good thing.

5. *What next?* Discuss what you think you might want to do with your results. Be clear about what action you will take, and what your next question might look like. This is critical to an action research disposition.

6. *Ask for feedback*. Again, don't be afraid. Ask for feedback on the project. What recommendations might others have for you? What criticisms might they have about what you did? What do people think you did well? There is no right or wrong in action research projects, this is an opportunity for development.

At its best, action research is a communal endeavor. A community of action researchers is worth more than the sum of its parts. As you model what you have done for your classmates or colleagues, ask for input and thoughts about the process. Make room for people to ask questions about your practice, and they will begin to question their own.

More questions? See questions 67 and 77.

How Do I Tell a Story With My Data?

A fter you have collected your data, there are two very important questions to ask about the distribution. The distribution is the relative number of times each observed outcome occurred in your dataset. You can think of an ordered list of scores in a single column in a table (or spreadsheet). Your story will focus on two attributes of that distribution: You will want to know (a) where the middle is and (b) how spread out the scores are from each other. These are important because they help you understand the nature of the scores in their entirety, not just the characteristics of a single score. These two key descriptors help you to understand the group of scores.

You already understand the middle of the distribution. It's called the average score, often called the *mean*. Knowing where the middle is helps you interpret how far away some scores might be, whether higher or lower. You can think of the mean of a distribution as what is closest to normal, because scores in your distribution tend to cluster around that mean. Knowing how a participant's single score compares to that mean is meaningful (pun intended). In some cases, you may ask for a different estimate of the middle, the *median*, or middle score.

The spreadoutedness helps us to understand, relative to the middle, how far away is really far. A simple way to think of this variation in your data is to isolate the bottom and top score—the *range*. For example, knowing the average score is 30 is meaningless without knowing the range of scores. Perhaps the average is 30, and the scores range from 20 to 40. Or perhaps the average is 30, and the scores range from 20 to 80. These are very different situations. Instead of the range, researchers usually use something akin to the average distance from the middle to describe the spreadoutedness. This is called a *standard deviation*. This is easy to calculate with spreadsheet software or on the Web. The standard deviation helps us understand the range of scores that is most normal. The middle told us approximately, and the standard deviation gives you more precision. For example, if you had the mean score of 50 and a standard deviation of 10, then 50, plus or minus 10, is the range in which most participants scored. Now you have a deeper understanding of what a normal score is; the range of 40 to 60 is most normal. This may be of interest to you, particularly if you are interested in identifying lower or higher performers.

What Is the Difference Between the Mean and Median, and Why Is It Important?

I n the preceding question, we touched on descriptive statistics. In particular, we distinguished between mean (the average) and median (the middle score). You might be asking, why is there more than one way to describe the middle of a distribution? Think about why the housing industry uses the median as an estimate of house values and not the mean. Likely, this is because there tend to be a few houses at the very high end of every market that drive the mean price higher, so it is not an accurate indication of what average home prices are, because it's not the true middle anymore.

The mean is generally an excellent way to estimate the middle. Take all the scores, add them up, and divide by the number of scores. Consider this set of data, as we make the distinction about when median might be more appropriate.

A	B
4	4
8	8
12	12
15	15
18	18
21	21
21	44
mean	14	17.5
median	15	15

Columns A and B have sets of scores from some measure we used. The scores are identical, except for the last. In Column A, the last score is 21, and in Column B, 44. The mean and median are at the bottom.

Note that the mean of column B (17.5) is much higher than column A (14). This is because of that one score of 44 pulling the mean up. This score is called an outlier, and it can impact the mean drastically. Typically, if a score is two standard deviations from the mean, it is considered an outlier. After all, most cluster around that median, not the higher mean score. A similar phenomenon would exist if there was an extremely low score in one column. The outliers are said to *skew* the distribution one way or another, negatively or positively. In contrast, the median score for both columns is the same. Now, considering the drastic impact of the outlier, the median is probably a better measure of where the middle is. Probably knowing both gives you the best idea of where the middle of the distribution is. With your project in particular, you will want to carefully look for outliers. One way to deal with this is to report your data twice, though it's probably easiest to note it and move on.

More questions? See question 75.

How Do Inferential Statistics Work?

We discussed the idea of conducting action research without inferential statistics and what that means to triangulation. While inferential statistics are not critical to action research, if you can do them, or have someone do them for you, we suggest you do.

Remember that descriptive statistics are different from inferential statistics. Inferential statistics allow you to compare your finding to what should have probably happened if you did nothing. In a nutshell, you compare your results to a probability distribution. If different enough, you can generalize to broader populations. To understand the question of what is *different enough*, you need to learn a little about statistical significance.

When you compare your results to a probability distribution, you are kind of hoping there is difference, because that means your treatment or intervention worked, and it wasn't just due to chance (probability). Statistical significance is an expression of this difference and how certain you are that there is difference. Most researchers in the social sciences agree that they need to be 95% confident their results are different than what might happen by chance. That's a high bar. In health sciences research, 99% and above can be found. If you do choose to try inferential statistics in your action research, 95% is probably your go-to.

More questions? See questions 63 and 65.

How Can I Use Inferential Statistics in My Action Research?

There are a few typical inferential statistics used in action research. Most are easily accessible through your regular spreadsheet software. You might be surprised to learn there are also freely accessible Web-based statistics calculators available. Let's look at the correlation, chi-square, and T-test.

- Correlations establish strength of relationships between two or more interval variables. We briefly discussed this in the context of research design. The correlation coefficient is expressed as (r). If the value is −1, there is a perfect negative relationship between the two variables; as one goes up, the other goes down. Not surprisingly, a value of +1 is a perfectly positive relationship; as one goes up, the other goes up. And values in between −1 and +1 indicate varying degrees of negative and positive relationships. A value of 0 means no relationship at all.

- Chi-square (χ^2) is a procedure that compares differences between groups on categorical variables. For example, you might ask, Do males smoke more than females? Here's what a table of the data might look like for a group of 30 people (15 each).

Comparison of Male and Female Smokers and Nonsmokers			
	Smoker	**Nonsmoker**	**Total**
Male	7	8	15
Female	11	4	15
Total	17	13	30

On the face of it, it looks like there are 11 female smokers and 7 male smokers, so you might conclude the opposite, that more females smoke than males. In typical action research, you might conclude just that. But if you wanted to generalize, you would use a chi-square analysis to determine if this difference was statistically different.

- With a T-test, you can compare one or two groups of people on continuous/interval variables to determine if there is a significant difference. There are three kinds:
    1. The *one-sample T-test* asks if the score you found is different than what you expected.
    2. The *independent samples T-test* compares two different groups of people on one measure.
    3. The *paired samples T-test* compares the same group on a given measure twice, like in a pretest/posttest design.

Other analyses that might interest the action research are analysis of variance (ANOVA), which unlike the T-test allows you to analyze more than two groups, and the linear regression analysis, which allows you to predict one variable with another.

More questions? See questions 75 and 79.

What Is an Effect Size, and Who Is Cohen?

E ffect size is a way of expressing the magnitude of the difference between two groups. In a nonstandardized setting, you might simply report the difference between two means. One group had an average 35, and one had an average 50, so the effect size is 15 points. You might also express it as percent change in a group. Perhaps one group grew from 55% to 75% on your measure. The effects size is 20%. Unfortunately, expressing effect size in raw units does not consider the importance of variance in the distribution. There is a not-so-tough way to do this.

Calculating a standardized effect size allows you to move beyond the simplistic "Does it work or not?" to the far more sophisticated "How well does it work in a range of contexts?" Moreover, by placing the emphasis on the most important aspect of an intervention—the size of the effect—rather than its statistical significance, it promotes a more scientific approach to the accumulation of knowledge. For these reasons, effect size is an important tool in reporting and interpreting effectiveness.

The most noted expert in the area of effect size is Cohen, and the statistic he developed to help express the magnitude of difference in research is called Cohen's *d*. There are other effect sizes out there in the world and, depending on your choice of statically analysis, you might want to use another, but Cohen's *d* is universally recognized by researchers.

Action researchers don't typically calculate effect size, but we recommend calculating it when possible. There are a ton of free calculators out there, and all that is necessary are your descriptive statistics. The beauty of Cohen's *d* is that it puts the effect size on a metric from 0 to 1. Cohen suggested categorizes effect sizes as small (<0.2), medium (.2–.8), and large (>.8), although he cautions that judgments depend on the purpose and context.

How Do I Deal With Missing Data?

You have collected your data, and now you need to analyze them. But first, you'll need some skill in cleaning them up and organizing them. It's common to use some spreadsheet software here, like Excel™, Google Sheets™, the Apache Open source Calc™, or on a Mac perhaps Numbers™. No matter which piece of software you choose to use, they all pretty much do the same thing. Rows and columns to organize the data you collected.

Typically, people are in rows, and the data you collected, variables like gender, ethnicity, some scores on a variable of interest, and group number if you used a group design, go in columns. Populating the cells in your spreadsheet can be tedious, but if you collected it with an online survey tool, that process can be automated. Or maybe you have a friend or child willing to work for potato chips? In a spreadsheet, your data might look like this:

ID	Group	Female	Score 1 (%)	Score 2 (%)
1	1	0	56	70
2	1	1	61	73
3	1	0	–	65
4	2	0	51	54
5	2	0	44	59
6	2	1	64	64

Note that instead of coding the participants as male or female, you can use a numerical value; the column female is coded as (1) for true and (0) for false. This is a good trick for a lot of variables. It is called *dummy coding* and makes data easier to analyze later. The mean of the female column is 0.33, which translates to 33% female.

The first thing you will notice after entering the data into your spreadsheet is that not all of the data are there. There will be empty cells. Perhaps you didn't have all the data, or someone wasn't there when you collected them, or the data collection tool didn't work for some reason. What you do with the empty cells where data can be missing is important. There are a few approaches. The most common, with small datasets, let's say less than 50, is to remove the person who has missing data. Delete the entire row. Another approach might be to impute an average score—in this case the average of the score 1 column is 55%, so we could substitute this. This approach is called treating empty cells *missing at random*. The other technique would be to look at the characteristics, or strata, of the empty cells and impute the average of all the others that shared these characteristics or were in the same strata. This is called *missing not at random*.

As you compile your dataset, you'll want to consider any identifying information you may have collected, especially names. Get rid of them as soon as possible. A good trick is to use ID numbers instead of names. If you need to come back later to match participants to subsequent data collection, you can create a second secure file that matches names to ID numbers. Naturally, you would keep this file in a different place on a different computer.

What Are Some Good Action Research Analytic Tools I Can Use?

One of the difficulties with conducting analyses is having access to intuitive software that is free. No one wants to (or typically can) pay for expensive software, or to a greater extent, wants to do it by hand. While many analytic tools exist, Google provides much of the power and action researchers need in one fell swoop for free. (No, this is not a plug for Google.)

- **Descriptive statistics.** Typically, the action researcher is not interested in generalizing the findings from their study to other settings, so complicated inferential statistics are generally unwarranted. Instead, depending on the project, the researcher is interested in counting (frequencies), finding middles (measures of central tendency), and understanding the variation in data—collectively known and measures of central tendency or descriptive statistics. Having said that, there are several tools with a rudimentary ability to calculate inferential statistics. Google Sheets is much like Excel. A distinct advantage is its ability to seamlessly merge with all of the free Google tools like Google Docs, Google Drive, and Google Forms. Apache and Microsoft both have Open Office suites that feature good spreadsheet software. Notably, the commonly used Excel is available.

- **Inferential statistics and effect size.** Inferential statistics are advanced statistics that are useful to determine probabilistic (quantitative) modeling to establish relationships (correlations), to infer causality (t-tests, ANOVAs), or to gauge the magnitude of the treatment (effect size). We really like the one from Social Science Statistics at www.socscistatistics.com. It has just about everything you will need to conduct statistical analyses without cost.

- **Qualitative data analysis.** Qualitative research, while potentially collecting numerical data, typically begins with written or audio recorded records from participants. The spreadsheets outlined above can work with numerical and textual data. Features like word frequency are ideal for discovering emergent and salient themes within large amounts of textual data. An advantage of using Google Calc is the integration of the Google Translate feature, which may be of benefit to many qualitative researchers working with multiple languages. Google Translate is not perfect but is better than nothing. A quick trick to determine the accuracy of the translation is to translate one way and then back, and to compare differences. In addition to spreadsheets, the qualitative researcher might also be interested in Google Cloud's Speech to Text tool, which enables the user to quickly and accurately move audio transcript of focus groups and interviews to text.

• **Survey creation tools.** Most survey tools feature the ability to analyze data, at least at the descriptive level. A key advantage is after the data are collected online, there is no need for the researcher to input data. A few clicks of the mouse, and the analysis is performed, and results are displayed in tables. Better tools feature the ability to display results graphically. We like Google Forms because it integrates so well with the rest of the Google tool family, like Docs, Sheets, and Translate. Qualtrics and Survey Monkey are noteworthy commercial products and are far more robust than Google Forms; however, the free versions of these provide limitations on the number of participants, number of questions in the survey, and limit the more advanced data analysis features.

More questions? See questions 88, 89, and 90.

Why Is Using Data Displays an Important Step?

S omeone once said a picture is worth a thousand words, and many have said it since. More than just efficient ways to convey information, they also allow for deeper analysis and reflection. Some patterns and relationships can be revealed with pictures, whether in table or figure. The line between the two has slowly been blurred as technology allows for hybrids, graphs that look like tables, tables that employ communicative graphics, and so on.

Traditionally, a table is thought of as a purposeful organization of text or numerical information in a grid of rows and columns, but more than a spreadsheet. The table contains summary data. Data are organized in such a manner as to encourage comparison.

Figures, like tables, enable you to convey a lot of information and opportunity for comparison without text. Graphs are particularly powerful tools, because you can decide what message you want to convey and build your graph to do it for you. Like graphs, charts can convey messages. Consider Figure 84.1. It should look familiar!

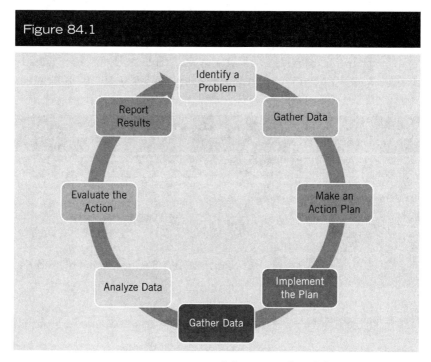

Figure 84.1

More questions? See question 67.

QUESTION

85

What Are the Elements of a Good Table?

G ood tables communicate data efficiently, perhaps in seconds. They typically focus on summary/aggregated data, not individual data points (with a few exceptions, e.g., single-case design methodology).

- The table layout should make sense and be easily understood. Try to use a standard-looking table, because this makes it easier for the reader to quickly find information. Novel tables can create confusion. Colors and shading are not always ideal.

- If possible, keep numbers that will be compared close to each other; these will be the ones most closely related to the research question, and it's OK to bold some or use italics to draw attention. Again, this makes it easier for the reader to get to the information quickly.

- Make your table easy on the eyes. White space is good. Using only horizontal lines is also a good idea, if you can do it. The white space serves as the vertical line.

Consider this example of an easy to read table. You may have already seen it in another question but pay closer attention to the recommendations above as you examine it now.

Comparison of Male and Female Smokers and Nonsmokers			
	Smoker	**Nonsmoker**	**Total**
Male	7	8	15
Female	11	4	15
Total	17	13	30

More questions? See questions 67 and 84.

What Are the Elements of a Good Graph?

A picture is worth a thousand words. Let's add to that axiom, a *good* picture is worth a thousand words. Data graphs can convey masses of information if they are designed well. When creating a graph to share your data, there are three important aspects that should be considered: accuracy, clarity, and efficacy. There is an extensive body of literature on this topic, but here are some of the highlights. In a nutshell, these guidelines help us to create graphs that convey nothing but information.

- **Accuracy**. Graphs should portray relationships accurately. Not just that the data points plotted accurately, but also the titles are clear and unambiguous, and that labels and descriptions appropriately tied to the data. The scale chosen to show the data should help the reader make connections and see relationships in the data.

- **Clarity**. In keeping with maintaining clarity in data graphics, scholars suggest avoiding the use of legends. Ideally data are directly labelled on the graph. Remove redundant axes, guiding tick marks, and graphics unrelated to the data (e.g., pictures).

- **Efficacy**. The scholar Tukey differentiated three kinds of data graphics. The first and the simplest form is a graph that takes the place of a table. This simple graph does nothing more than portray data and promotes nothing more than reading unadorned values. The second kind of graph, the propaganda graph, is used to convey a particular message to the graph reader. In this case, the graph directs the reader toward a predetermined conclusion. The third and the most valuable graph is the analytic graph, designed to elicit exploration, contemplation, and comparison.

More questions? See questions 67 and 84.

How Do I Evaluate the Quality of My Action Research Project?

Be it in business, health science, education, or the social sciences, action research is about influencing behavior to improve outcomes. And steps to those improved outcomes are identifying a problem, determining a strategy, collecting and analyzing data, and planning for action. But how do you know if you're doing the right thing? There are four big questions to ask yourself when you finish a project.

1. **Can I trust the results?** This is a matter of questioning validity, or the trustworthiness of your results. We discussed extensively concepts of reliability and validity, as well as potential controls for threats in earlier questions. If you can trust your results, you can safely say that your resulting decisions are good ones.

2. **Did my project benefit stakeholders?** Stakeholders are not just those directly participating in you research, but the community at large too. For example, you might share your project with colleagues, who might also be stakeholders. And this is an important point. Action research isn't just for the sake of research; its key benefits are consumable and relevant to the researcher and broader community.

3. **Did it benefit your practice?** The ultimate answer is to change or affirm something you're doing. In the Action Research Cycle, the final step is asking yourself how you might improve further, and to answer that question you need to fully understand the change that occurred and the potential for change. Action research is ongoing. If the change didn't work, what should you do to change that? If it did, what can you do to improve further? And the cycle continues.

4. **Was it worth your time?** There is a cost to everything, notably time and money. It's important to evaluate that cost relative to its benefit. This can only be answered by you.

More questions? See questions 7 and 8.

PART 9

Action Research in the Bigger World

You don't create a box and put people in and then make a lot of generalizations about them.

—Clarence Thomas

Now That I Am Done, How Do I Add Value to the Field?

F irst, share with colleagues to improve practice. This might happen in morning huddles, faculty meetings, or sales meetings. It's important to be frank and open about what you have done, what you're doing, and what you're going to do. Beyond simply sharing findings, you're building a culture of inquiry, and in that culture, you are fostering a growth mindset. Second, after building local buy-in, share with the field in general. There are many ways to do this. Below we list potential outlets in order from easiest to hardest for sharing. *Important note*: You are not sharing only data or results (unless you have permission); you will want to share experiences and wisdom, and maybe get some along the way.

- **Social media**. Is exactly what it says it is. Social media consists of websites or applications that allow participants to share content and participate in conversation, for example, Facebook, Twitter, YouTube, Instagram, and so on. These outlets are typically tailored to more individualized preferences, and no oversite or moderation is maintained.

- **Blogs**. Blogs are regularly maintained websites where contributions typically converse on a given topic. The participatory nature of blogs creates a more formal outlet than social media to share your work with the world, and they are typically moderated by an individual or group that has a vested interest in that particular topic.

- **Journals**. There are several action research journals out there. In fact, Sage has its own, *Action Research*. Each journal comes with different submission requirements, but if your action research project is done with fidelity, these journals are also excellent outlets.

So, this was a trick question. Your action research project is never done. The findings of your action research project generate new questions. It might be a refinement to increase precision of the initial question, an adjustment to the parameters and measures, some gained insight not planned for but emerged, or a realization that your question was completely irrelevant. Remember the Action Research Cycle. The last step is to look at your question and decide where to go from there.

More questions? See question 90.

What Professional Organizations Are Available to Give Me Support?

Depending on your field, there might be different organizations that might support your work. We'll give you a look at the social sciences, health care, and business.

In the social sciences, including education:

- *American Educational Research Association (AERA)*

  AERA is the world's largest educational research organization. There is ample room for professional development and though colleagues project support. AERA has several special interest groups (SIG) dedicated to action research, including the aptly named *Action Research SIG*, and the *Research to Use SIG*. A good way to start would be to attend the annual convention, network with like-minded people, and attend relevant sessions.

- *Association for Supervision and Curriculum Development (ASCD)*

  ASCD is a practitioner-oriented organization made up of teachers, school counselors, and school administrators. They publish several short texts on action research, but more importantly, the furthering of inquiry-oriented education is one of the organization's fundamental tenets.

- *American Psychological Association (APA)*

  APA explicitly supports the use of action research in the social sciences. They devote a part of their website to "Research in Action," a repository of action research studies from the field. Through the website, APA promotes the use of *action science* in everyday lives. This organization is enormous and attending the annual convention will provide a new action researcher with plenty of experience and insights.

In the health sciences:

- *American Nurses Association (ANA)*

  ANA is the largest national nursing organization with local offices throughout many states. Benefits to members includes access to an extensive online library for information and up-to-date research, and specialty webinars offering additional contact hours.

- *Hospice and Palliative Nurses Association (HPNA)*

  HPNA is an organization that specializes in hospice and end-of-life care. This is an excellent network that provides mentorship and support for those who work with terminal patients. HPNA is also a great way to gain leadership and collaboration skills.

- *National Student Nurses Association (NSNA)*

  NSNA is an organization that specializes in student nurses. It provides educational and employment services and resources, and offers a wide variety of educational, leadership skill-building, and networking opportunities for those entering the field. The organization supports the professional development of student nurses in areas like ethics and research scholarship.

In business and industry:

- *Management Study Guide (MSG)*

  MSG is a global organization that provides practical learning and instructional modules on business management–related topics, including action research. Members have access to practical instruction related to up-to-date industry needs that are conducted by MSG experts in education and industry. All modules are job oriented and skill based.

- *Project Management Institute (PMI)*

  PMI is a professional development organization in project management. Members have access to mentorship and networking opportunities through live events and seminars, and webinars, as well as access to organizational publications and tools for project management.

- *American Marketing Association (AMA)*

  AMA is a cutting-edge association that uses action research to leverage marketing as a critical piece to business enterprises. AMA also offers members differentiated content focusing on best marketing practices and publishes scholarly journals that welcome action research.

More questions? See question 90.

Are Social Media Outlets Appropriate for Sharing My Action Research?

The answer is yes *and* no, depending on what you share. Social media outlets, online networks designed to connect people to each other, are designed to help people share information and ideas. This is great for things like news, reporting on events, rallying people to a cause, and watching new cat videos. The greatest benefit is that it promotes more equal access to information when shared. Of course, that doesn't mean it is good, valid, and true information, something we all need to be aware of when using social media. It also doesn't mean all information is shared. Thus, social media might have some beneficial societal impact, but it cannot be the only outlet.

Social media does have the potential to connect practitioners engaged in action research, to facilitate sharing of research questions, methodologies, and results. This can be beneficial to the action researcher; however, stakeholders and participants may not see it the same way. There is a real danger that personal information and data might be inadvertently shared. And once on in the social media Internet space, there is really no perfect way of getting it back. As a general rule, it is fine to share your project questions and methodology, but not to share results on social media.

More questions? See question 88.

91

Can I Formally Publish My Action Research Project?

Publishing research can be a prestigious activity and may lead to scholarly or career advancement. Publishing research can also come with high accolades, but not always. Understanding what moderates the quality of research is key to sharing your research, but also consuming others' research. Remember that journals vary in quality and their procedures for reviewing submitted studies. It would behoove you to find a couple of journals (maybe even those you used in your literature synthesis) that align with your needs. If you choose to formally submit to a scholarly journal, here are a few general guidelines to follow.

- **Style**. Different journals use different styles. Three typical styles are APA, MLA, and Chicago. Although most journals rely on APA, each journal is different. It would be good to check with the journal before getting too far into it (hint: it's usually on the journal website). Whichever style is required, there are many online tools to help you get it right.

- **Format**. Typical scholarly journals follow a standard formula with four primary parts: Introduction, Methods, Results, Discussion. Commit to memory: IMRD. If you conducted a literature review, you are probably familiar with this format, but it bears explicit description.

  - *Introduction*: The introduction frames the problem under investigation in light of your context, contains a formal literature synthesis, and ends with your research question or hypothesis.

  - *Methods*: This is the meat of your study. It's where you describe your participants (who your participants were), materials (what you used), procedures (how you conducted your study), and the data analytic approach (how you intended to analyze your data). Internal validity is also discussed in this section.

  - *Results*: This is a dry section full of technical language where you tell the reader what your analyses yielded. Basically, no adjectives. This section is full of tables and graphs.

o   *Discussion*: This is where your voice comes in. You summarize for the reader in layperson language what you found and why you think you found it. Finally, you link this back to your introduction and, voila, you are finished.

- **Submission**. After finding an applicable journal, determining style, and complying to format requirements, it's time to submit. Usually, in peer-reviewed journals, authors are required to submit a title sheet without author attribution (this facilitates blind peer review), a copyright waiver (the journal owns your work once it's published), and the manuscript. The editor will respond pretty quickly if the manuscript is appropriate for the journal, but then it typically takes 1–2 months to receive feedback. You will get one of three decisions: accepted without revisions (if this happens re-look at the quality of the journal), accepted with revisions (this is typical; be sure to address review feedback explicitly), and rejected (hey, it happens). If you get rejected, don't worry. If you can address reviewer feedback, it will make it stronger in your secondary journal submission.

More questions? See question 77.

92

What Are the Most Helpful Action Research Journals?

One of the difficulties in accessing action research or research in general is a system of journals that charge for content. Authors don't get paid to publish their studies in journals, but many journals turn around and charge readers to access the research. This poses an obstacle for many. The main advantage to this system of information distribution is the establishment of high-quality research in journals, whether print or digital. Most require all proposals be vetted by experts in the field before being published. The easiest way to gain access to research that is behind a money firewall is to go to your local university library. Many, especially large universities, have already paid for access to the journals and provide free access to the public.

Whether you want to read action research or publish your own research, the following are our recommendations:

Journal	Description
Action Research/ Cross-discipline	*AR* sits at the forefront of the field. It has been published since 2003 by Sage (us.sagepub. com). Its mission is to provide an alternative to traditional research outlets. They refer to traditional research as being disinterested in alternative models. Clearly the journal supports and builds upon the idea that action research is valued.
Educational Action Research/Education	*EAR* is tailored for those interested in the application of action research to the field of education. The journal aims to bridge research and practice, a known gap in the field of education.
Action Research & Action Learning Journal/ Cross-discipline	*ARALJ* describes and analyzes the use of action research as it relates to social and organizational change. This flagship journal is tied to the broader organization that promotes generating learning, training, and research for social justice.

Journal	Description
International Journal for Transformative Research/ Cross-discipline	*IJTR* aims to transform research by challenging the status quo of traditional research and thereby create change in society—novel and innovative thinking and research in social, political, and educational arena.
Journal of Applied Behavioral Science/Social sciences	*JABS* seeks to address issues that concern a diversity of audiences, and publishes material designed to help people promote positive change. The journal explores group dynamics, organizational development, and social change in a broad range of fields, but primarily psychology.
Journal of Organizational Change Management/ Business & industry	*JOCM* strives to provide a venue for publishing alternative philosophies for organizational change and organizational change management. It publishes both qualitative and quantitative approaches.
Management Learning/ Business & industry	*ML* publishes articles that move away from descriptive and traditional research methods. They emphasize critique and critical thinking. The editors support alternative research methods, like action research.
Health Education Journal/ Health care	*HEJ* primarily publishes traditional research, but the journal has a history of being open to action research projects, too. The journal focuses on health education research, a great fit for action research.

Should I Repeat (Replicate) My Action Research Project?

With action research, you are generally not interested in replicating because you are primarily interested in understanding what works in *your* practice, not others'. However, there are conditions when it might be desirable.

Replicating a study means repeating it using the same methods and under the same condition, but with different participants and perhaps a different researcher. If you are interested in generalizing your findings, replication is a good idea. It helps you to more convincingly argue that your results are reliable and your decisions are valid. It helps to control for extraneous variables that you could not account for previously, and if successful, it implies that your method is applicable to different situations, which can further research in the field. Replication primarily lets others know that the innovation can work in different places for different people and also inspires others to improve on your innovation. It is always best to start with something we know that works, and then work toward improvement.

An ideal use of a replication study is when you have been asked to adopt an innovation previously researched. For example, as a nurse, you may be asked to adjust dosage levels of some medication. You know that research indicates optimal dosage levels, and you in the course of your work adhere to the recommendations. This does not preclude you from collecting data on the implementation. Find the original study that indicated optimal dosage levels and do it again in the course of your work. You are not changing the dosage; you care replicating and confirming findings. Does it apply equally to the community you are serving? Sometimes that answer is yes, but that answer depends on factors not controlled for in the original study.

More questions? See question 75.

Future Steps

If we knew what it was we were doing, it would not be called research, would it?

—**Albert Einstein**

94

Is Action Research in Any Way Political? How Do I Navigate That?

In higher education, action research is typically looked down upon from the more positivist light, because the institution's perspective is that action research doesn't offer the same rigor as traditional research. Action research does not focus on theory building or adding to the body of knowledge; rather it aims to improve practice directly, which is contrary to institutional traditions and priorities.

Be it a teacher, nurse, or web developer in a cubicle, moving from research to practice can be challenging. However, there are multiple dimensions in which to work. First, understand that action research is inherently political and fraught with power dynamics, cultural (mis)understandings, and consequences. Work to define and engage those relationships during the process. This builds trust and goes a long way to lending credibility to your findings and potential action. Second, know who is involved. Knowledge produced from action research projects isn't intended to be transferred to others for implementation, like objectivist (outsider) research, but rather to include those directly involved with making change. Know these stakeholders and give them a voice. Partnerships that are rooted in trust, buy-in, and active participation can help you navigate the political scene.

QUESTION

95

How Can I Create an Inquiry-Oriented Disposition in My Everyday Life?

Using an inquiry-oriented disposition means keeping an *open mind*: Ask a question, make a hypothesis, consider a research method, test the hypothesis, reach a conclusion, and revise the question. In essence, this is critical thinking. Asking questions with well-defined parameters is the beginning step in the process of understanding strengths and weaknesses of practices used. Collecting data before and after innovations, partitioning that data to more fully understand the impact, monitoring fidelity of implementation, and controlling for threats to validity are all part of inquiry-oriented practice. When this inquiry disposition becomes a habit of mind and practice, you are an action researcher. Creating and fostering a culture of inquiry means modeling action research behavior: Model reflection, the pursuit of expertise, and willingness to share.

- **Deep reflection.** If you never ask what you might be doing poorly, you will always do it poorly. In education, the traditional model puts a principal in a classroom evaluating teacher performance, maybe once a year for a couple of hours. Can we honestly say that works well? Two avenues of evaluation should always be present in practices—the obvious one concerned with workplace success and growth, and the less obvious one focused on personal growth. Guided with a research-based disposition, practitioners think more critically about themselves and their role.

- **The pursuit of expertise.** Excellent leaders love leading, and they have a genuine curiosity about what makes a good leader. At the heart of this curiosity is a willingness to accept that they are not perfect and may never be perfect. Leaders should pursue expertise in two ways—first, expert knowledge of the content in which they work, and second, expert knowledge of how to develop that knowledge.

- **Sharing knowledge and experiences.** Improvement cannot be arrived at in isolation. Collaboration and sharing can take place in three equally important areas. Within the workplace, you can create both formal and informal communities of practice and networks of knowledge. Collaboration and sharing provide opportunities for communal learning between and among action researchers and your stakeholders. Collaboration with the community completes the sharing circuit.

More questions? See question 9.

Why Develop an Action Research Community?

An action research community typically refers to the interactive relationships between colleagues with the intent on improving practice through action research. The community meets often and commits to central tenets. The community has

- central and clear vision in common,
- shared values and purpose,
- collective focus on ethical and responsible improvement,
- shared drive to collaborate,
- willingness to share experiences and results of action research,
- shared control in significant organizational decision making, and
- respect for all ideas.

A caveat. Groups of people mutually interested in some kind of improvement can often agree that an action research approach is sound; however, they have difficulty agreeing on an area of action research worthy of the entire group. For example, practitioners at a community dental center can all agree that promoting and creating better dental health is the shared goal. At the same time, individuals may have very different ideas on how to improve practice. Do they want to investigate the quality of bedside manner? Do they want to investigate the impact of an investment in new equipment? Perhaps a professional development initiative?

A fruitful starting point is for individuals to design and conduct their own action research, and then to share findings with broader group. As more individuals engage in action research, it builds a culture of action researchers. Think of this as a grassroots approach to building the action research community.

More questions? See questions 88 and 95.

Why Would I Want or Need to Write a Report on My Action Research?

A teacher once described the process of having to write up results from an action research project as "a complete waste of time." We hope that isn't the case, but we can understand that perspective. Let's face it. Most of us are eager to just get into the meat of research and do it. You want to ask a question about your practice and then answer it. You want to make changes to improve your own life and those of the people you serve. So, if you are simply interested in improving your own practice, how would documenting the process and results be of any use? There are several answers.

Writing a formal (or informal) report on what you did, why you did it, and what happened as a result forces you to clarify and evaluate the Action Research Cycle. Writing is thinking. For example, by having to write down who your students, patients, or customers are, you are forced to examine how they are similar or different. By synthesizing recent literature on similar questions, you are enabling yourself to reflect on what others have done and how you might do it differently. By having to write down how you will implement an innovation, you are forced to create fidelity within that innovation. In essence, you create consistency in the way you do it. By writing up your results, creating tables and charts, you are forced to examine the resulting data in creative and more meaningful ways. And finally, when you write a reflection of the process, you are forcing yourself to answer questions like *What went well? What didn't go well? What would I have done differently?* And perhaps most importantly, *how should I ask that question in a more meaningful way if I were to do it again?*

Simply put, action researchers are not *just* interested in improving practice. While it may serve as the driving force when asking and answering questions, it is not the sole factor. You are interested in helping all of your stakeholders, and so, sharing your story can benefit others. This is often done with a simple discussion. However, more formal documentation of the effort is more likely to lead to affecting change outside your locus of control.

More questions? See questions 91 and 92.

What Are the Key Elements of an Action Research Report?

When you do write up your action research project, there are some key elements to consider. Much of this book explored these in more detail. Broadly, these components are the following:

- **Decide on an area of improvement/focus**. The area of improvement is naturally driven by questions you have about your practice. You see an area that needs improvement or change, and you think to yourself, what if I did something different?

- **Review recent literature and refine your question.** When you know what you want to work on, you really should look to see if others have asked and answered that question already. You might start with a simple Web search for relate articles. Google Scholar is an excellent resource for finding research studies. You may discover that you question was too simplistic, or worse, too general. Reviewing recent literature will help you to understanding salient variables. These can help you refine and create a meaningful research question that will yield more useful information.

- **Create a statement of your procedure**. Now that you know what question to ask, you'll need to decide how to best answer that question. What will you do, and how will you do it? How often will you do it, and for how long? Who will you do it to? How will you collect data to reflect changes? How do you think you will analyze those data?

- **Collect those data**! This is the fun part of action research. Maybe you are conducting observations, or maybe you are using a pre- and posttest design. Perhaps you have decided to develop a series of survey.

- **Analyze your data**. During and after your analysis prepare a summary of results and create data visualizations to explore the data.

- **Reflect on these results and develop a new action plan**. Will you stop something? Will you continue? Will you change? Did you ask the right question? These are the possible outcomes of the reflection process and will lead to some kind of action, which inevitably returns you to the beginning of the Action Research Cycle, composing (or recomposing) a research question.

More questions? See questions 31 and 32.

I Really Liked Learning About Action Research. What Is Next?

In the academy, action research is not always respected. Institutions of higher education focus on rigorous experimental research design (traditional research). Action research is about participating in your own research, intimately. Where might you go next? There are some options.

One clear-cut path is to continue to pursue higher education. This is not a venue for improving action research, but instead a way to learn more about what we like to call the *dark side*. We are kidding, of course. We took that path and don't regret a moment of it. It is worth noting not all universities have a research focus. Since 1970, the Carnegie Commission on Higher Education has been ranking universities in terms of their focus on research.

For master's degrees, the Commission rates them simply on the number of degrees awarded, which might be a good indicator of research activity. For doctoral programs, it is closely aligned with the quantity of research activity taking place, the number of research scholarships offered, and the annual number of graduating doctoral students from the university. They rank schools as Research 1, 2, or 3. Which one might fit you?

Not only are there courses in research methods at universities, including program evaluation, action research, qualitative methods, and quantitative methods, but there are entire programs that only teach research methods. Maybe this appeals you?

R1: Highest research activity

R2: Higher research activity

R3: Moderate research activity

More questions? See questions 89 and 90.

What Other Books in This Series Might Interest Me, and How Do They Fit Together?

The 100 Questions (and Answers) series bridges gaps between what traditional textbooks address and what you might want to know quickly. The most important questions are answered succinctly, for both novice and senior researchers. Currently (as of the year this book was published), the series includes seven books.

> *Research Methods* by Neil Salkind covers traditional research methods. It is the core text of the series. The Q&As begin with an introductory section and quickly move into formal research questions and methodologies. It can serve as an overview of the other texts in this series, and a terrific resource for someone considering an area of focus. It concludes with an overview if inferential statistics, which is continued in more detail in the next book by the same author, *100 Questions (and Answers) About Statistics.*

> *Statistics* by Neil Salkind begins with the basic Q&As about statistics, and moves though descriptive statistics, hypothesis testing, inferential statistics, and advanced group designs and procedures. This is an ideal companion to a more traditional textbook, or an introduction/ refresher for someone needing to get a brief answer to the most pressing questions in statistics.

> *Qualitative Research* by Lisa Given begins with foundational Q&As about the nature of qualitative research and follows with comprehensive and succinct Q&As about specific methods common in the field, with a special emphasis on research traditions and ethics.

> *Survey Research* by Erin Ruel provides a detailed set of Q&As about data collection techniques for large groups. From your initial sample selection to question writing, survey design, data analysis, and final report writing.

Tests and Measurement by Bruce Frey explores validity, reliability, test, and item construction across a broad array to test types, including the big four: intelligence, achievement, classroom-based, and personality tests.

Research Ethics by Emily Anderson and Amy Corneli covers Q&As about detailed aspects of ethics including the potential for participant risk, protecting confidentiality, protecting vulnerable populations, informed consent, and the formal process of obtaining research authorization from an internal review board. The Q&As are an excellent resource for new researchers, or those with experience looking to brush up on the modern complexities in this evolving area.

Action Research by Luke Duesbery and Todd Twyman provides Q&As about a younger and more dynamic research approach that puts the researcher into the research itself. The Q&As provide an important roadmap to guide practitioners to conduct rigorous research in their local context and is an excellent resource for individuals who wish to affect change and bridge the traditional research to practice gap.

The texts, while focusing on different facets of research, are in many ways complementary. Once you read one and understand how the *100 Questions (and Answers)* approach clearly and efficiently presents what you need know, you will want to read others in the series.

On a final note, the authors of this volume approached the publishers about writing this book after reading and using the others in their own courses. This is testament to the quality and usefulness of the series.

Appendix

Important Action Research Literature

Many scholars have emerged as action research has become popular and more mainstream. It continues to grow and gain momentum. We recommend to following *classics* as a sound foundation.

Lewin, G. W. (Ed.) (1948)
Resolving Social Conflicts
Harper & Row

Kurt Lewin is the pioneer of action research. He is often credited with coining the term *action research*. As early as the 1940s, he was arguing that there was a disconnect between traditional research and practice. He believed that by empowering practitioners with research tools, they could more effectively exact change. Lewin was the first to propose a cyclical approach to research, much like the Action Research Cycle (ARC) posited in this book.

Argyris, C. (1970)
Intervention Theory and Method: A Behavioral Science View.
Addison-Wesley

In the 1950s and 1960s, there was a decline in the prevalence of action research in the literature. There really isn't a particular reason, although it could be argued that social structures at the time didn't have support or resources necessary to conduct action research. It resurfaced in the 1970s with Argyris and an assortment of colleagues. They took a sociological approach to form a vision of action research, which included both unconscious and conscious decision making. They argued that people unconsciously design their actions to achieve desired outcomes and they naturally evaluate the efficacy of their efforts. Argyris would continue his work on what is called "double loop" learning until his death in 2013.

Schon, D. (1984)
The Reflective Practitioner: How Professionals Think in Action
Basic Books

In the 1980s, the work of Donald Schon extended his earlier collaborative work with his seminal work *The Reflective Practitioner*, where he believed self-reflection was key to learning. This closely parallels modern versions of action research, which hold that critical reflection leads to improved outcomes in the long term.

Greenwood, D. J., & Levin M. (2006)
Introduction to Action Research: Social Research for Social Change
Sage

In the 1990s action research saw its way into many disciplines. This was a time of spreading out for action research. Morten Levin was involved with groundbreaking work in the 1990s applying action research ideas to the integration of technology and organizational theory. In a nutshell, Morten argued that action research was the path to successful organizational change.

Index

Page references followed by (figure) indicate an illustrated figure.